TREVOR BEER'S
WILDLIFE OF NORTH DEVON

Trevor Beer

DEVON BOOKS

First published in Great Britain in 2001

Copyright © 2001 Trevor Beer

DEDICATION
*To Bracken, my dog and friend
who shared all of this with me, bless him.*

British Library Cataloguing-in-Publication Data
A CIP record for this title is available from the British Library

ISBN 1 85522 803 3
Catalogue data is available from the British Library

DEVON BOOKS
OFFICIAL PUBLISHER TO DEVON COUNTY COUNCIL
an imprint of

HALSGROVE
PUBLISHING, MEDIA AND DISTRIBUTION

Halsgrove House
Lower Moor Way
Tiverton, Devon EX16 6SS
Tel: 01884 243242
Fax: 01884 243325
email sales@halsgrove.com
website www.halsgrove.com

Printed in Italy by Grafiche D'Auria

Contents

Foreword by Tony Soper   5

Introduction   7

Author's Note   9

Spring   10

Summer   54

Autumn   108

Winter   137

Gazetteer   162

Lesser celandines carpet many a North Devon woodland as one of the heralds of springtime, from March and through the spring months they bring their cheery golden 'stars' to North Devon.

Foreword by Tony Soper

In these days when it is only too easy to slope off to Brittany for the weekend or to Disneyland for the annual holiday or even, perish the thought, one of the several annual holidays, it is a privilege to honour a man who patrols his muddy patch on a regular day-by-day basis.

Trevor Beer delights in recording the natural world on and around his native North Devon territory. And here in these pages is the perfect response to those people who wonder aloud 'how is it possible to walk the same way so many times without being terminally bored?' For of course the truth is that, in nature, change is constant and the challenge of unravelling the complexities of that change is what makes Trevor Beer such an entertaining companion.

Over the years our paths have crossed a number of times. And I am now struck by the thought that here, in the North Devon of yet another turn of the century, we have the reincarnation of Henry Williamson – the man who wrote three-quarters of a century ago in a style which combined ruthless observation with poetic insight. Trevor Beer has his eyes wide open, but his delight in the things he sees and hears comes straight from the heart. Too much natural history writing these days is mock-science, too much of the wildlife on the telly is technically superb but emotionally barren. This book offers an antidote.

One of the daily pleasures of the *Western Morning News* for which Trevor writes his regular columns is to wonder what blossom Trevor will pick from the tree of living things. Here, bound between the covers is a cornucopia of pleasures representing the wanderings with one of our most engaging guides. Once you dip into it, you will be transported into a real world, in the company of one of the fast disappearing breed of poet-naturalists.

Tony Soper
2001

A wild Exmoor combe. There are still many places in North Devon where we can find peace and solitude, with Exmoor one of the finest for beauty and wildlife in all England. About one-third of Exmoor lies in Devon.

Introduction

This book explores this beautiful part of the West Country through the eyes of a naturalist observing the four seasons across a typical year. Beginning with the first signs of spring we will find a countryside we all know well yet many rarely see in close-up, or as seasonal changes occur to some of the wild plants and creatures.

North Devon has a mix of habitats. Rivers, streams and estuary, farmland, woods and marshes, moorland and coast, all beautiful, all different, and providing a richness and diversity of wildlife that makes nature-watching a lifelong pursuit and pastime for all ages.

This book is timeless. It is a celebration of the countryside, its wildlife of past, present and future in full colour, with a text which follows the scenes across the year. It may be about North Devon yet it could be about many parts of England, any place, indeed, where the continuity of the seasons can be enjoyed with all one's senses.

Inevitably, in such a rich and diverse wildlife area as North Devon much has been left out but I hope readers will find as good a mix as space allows and forgive this writer for omissions. Perhaps another time…

Trevor Beer
Barnstaple
June 2001

Dog and bitch otters enjoying a quiet moment.

Author's Note

Devon County Council are very much to the fore in promoting nature conservation, often in partnership with the RSPB, Wildlife Trusts, English Nature and The Environment Agency for example. They have a County Ecology Officer on staff and currently have projects to protect culm grasslands, hedgerows, the primrose as part of a county survey, and of course initiated the now famous 'Tarka Project' as part of green tourism in Devon. The County Council also hosts the Devon Environmental Business Initiative (DEBI) which promotes environmental and conservation awareness with an annual award scheme involving wildlife conservation, recycling, and waste disposal aspects of business enterprise. Particularly important in recent years is the Devon Hedge Group linked with FWAG (Farming & Wildlife Advisory Group). The North Devon and Torridge District Councils, with the DCC, are currently involved in Biodiversity Action Plans in the North Devon Region, following the Rio Summit on the global environment several years ago. The Biodiversity Committees involved all sections of the public at the outset, with wildlife being part and parcel of this particular thrust to benefit the flora and fauna of the area as part of the web of life involving us all.

The RSPB and Devon Wildlife Trust offices are in Exeter, with branches in North Devon which have excellent programmes of indoor events and outdoor field trips. English Nature's Devon offices are at Okehampton and the Environment Agency is based at Exeter. British Butterfly Conservation has a Devon Branch which now includes a new moth group, whilst the British Naturalist Association also has a Taw and Torridge Branch with organised field trips. There is also the Devon Birdwatching and Preservation Society with its lively local branches. A trip to a local library will provide the reader with the relevant address and phone number of these and other organisations, such as the National Trust, who are all benefiting wildlife and the countryside in one way or another.

All in all the public need never be bored for there is so much to do. Becoming involved with nature conservation directly benefits wildlife and habitats, all part of the natural beauty and interest of North Devon's superb countryside.

Trevor Beer
June 2001

Chestnut

Spring

Primroses – their delicate perfume so much a part of springtime and of our Devon hedgebanks and broadleaved woodlands. The lent rose, butter rose, and darling of April are but three West Country names for this harbinger of spring; my favourite wildflower.

It is late March. The spring equinox has arrived. Clocks have been moved forward by one hour. We have gained the longer daylight hours and lighter nights allowing us more time to see and enjoy the splendours of nature. North Devon is awakening to the spring in its own subtle manner, gently throwing off the sleepy blanket of winter, gently yet purposefully for chiff-chaffs have arrived in woodlands awash with lesser celandines. The first primroses of the year, the prima rosas, peep from Devon hedgebanks along with dog violets and we know, no matter how hard winter may struggle to remain, there is an inevitable warming force of nature stirring every plant and creature as the new season begins.

Broadleaved woodlands are carpeted with lesser celandines, richly gold, shining in the sunlight. Used as a medicinal herb for a variety of maladies, including jaundice, piles, warts and the king's evil, Culpepper, the 17th century physician, cured his own daughter from the 'king's evil' using this little wild-flower, within a week, leaving no scars. An old country name is figwort.

North Devon names for the plant include brighteyes, butter-and-cheese, cream-and-butter, kingcup and starflower. Kingcup of course is also another name for marsh marigolds. Celandines (p.4) are also known as swallow herb, possibly because they flower when the swallows arrive back with us for the summer, although another belief is that they used the herb to strengthen the eyesight of their young. Interestingly the plant was used for human eye ailments. Hung over cow byres it was said to produce a high tide of cream in a cow's udder, provided the plant was picked at a flowing tide time, never at ebb. It is a member of the buttercup family, its scientific name being *Ranunculus ficaria*, 'ranunculus' the latin for 'little frog', denoting perhaps the plant's liking for moist places. Another story tells us Ranunculus was a young boy who wore green and yellow and who sang each day to the wood nymphs. One day, tiring of his singing they turned him into the flower.

The primrose (p.12) is the butter rose or lent rose in Devon, and is currently a 'flagship' plant of nature conservation, with Devon County Council conducting surveys because of its decline. It may appear to be common still, but many of its old haunts have disappeared.

The dog violet (p.18) is the scentless *Viola riviniana*, whilst the sweet violet, *V. odorata* is well known for its perfume 'Devon Violets'. Oil of violets and syrup of violets, cool and soothing in every way, are also products of this little plant.

Already the estuaries of the West Country, for months so full of the sounds of wintering waders and wildfowl, are quietening as many thousands of these birds leave for their breeding haunts about the globe. In North Devon the estuaries of the Taw and Torridge rivers, which both rise on Dartmoor to wend their separate ways over moorland and farmland, become spring migratory bird routes, the incoming and outgoing birds passing as ships in the night.

The largest human settlements on these two rivers are both on the intertidal waters, Bideford with the Torridge, Barnstaple a few miles distant on the Taw, the estuary a Site of Special Scientific Interest (SSSI) for its wader and wild-fowl importance both nationally and internationally. Known to many as 'sister' towns, Bideford with its working quayside and famous regatta, Barnstaple with its ancient annual fair, the two attract thousands of tourists many of whom come to enjoy the natural history of the area.

For the people of North Devon such matters are part of their own heritage and continuity, traditions as seasonal as nature's own, as much as the game of 'conkers' popular when horse chestnut fruits ripen, or blackberrying in late summer, harvesting we can all enjoy as farmers reap the harvests of their own toil and effort.

And so, as waders, wildfowl, starlings, wood pigeons, redwings and fieldfares depart to return to countries they fled in the depths of winter, back come our warblers, swallows, swifts and martins and the sound of the cuckoo is heard once again in the land. Misty tidal creeks such as those at Fremington and Braunton villages see the last of the redshanks leave as wheatears silently arrive to feed up after their long journeys from Africa and Mediterranean regions. A chiff-chaff sings the very first song of spring migrants from a treetop perch below which blackbirds have already begun to nest, their songs merging as the first dawn chorus of the year.

Blackie was our country name for the blackbird (p.37), common in garden and countryside. Where there are sheltered spots they will nest early, often raising three broods in a year. Its old name was Ouzel. It is the male who has the black plumage, the bright gold beak and eye-ring, the female being brown, the young rufous and speckled for a while. Thomas Hardy described the beak of the male as its 'crocus coloured bill', an apt description for it is an intense yellow in the breeding season. Its song is arguably the most beautiful of all British birds, the lovely flow of mellow notes enchanting. To 'whistle like a blackbird' means to do something easily, without effort.

Bideford regatta

An old saying that when a blackbird sings before Christmas she will cry before Candlemas suggests that if the birds nest too early along will come a cold snap and the eggs or young may be lost.

Several country names for birds were part of the North Devon dialect used by locals. I knew the wren as crackie, the blue tit as tomtit and ackymal, the moorhen as a dipchick. Some still use these names today, with herons quite commonly called cranes by older country folk.

The chiff-chaff is usually the first summer warbler to arrive and sing, a true herald of spingtime named from its two piercing notes wherever it is found. In Germany it is the zilp zalp. A Devon name is choice-and-cheep, whilst its nest gives it the names of bank bottle, feather poke and wood oven. Other country names include least whitethroat, lesser pettychaps and thummie. These old country names for birds often tell more about their ways than do names in current usage.

The trees which offer them both food and shelter now have sap rising within, their leaf buds ready to burst open to the warming sun, to turn the landscape green. An acorn (p.28) buried by a grey squirrel in last year's autumn sends up a shoot to explore the world of its parent tree. With good fortune on its side it will become a full grown oak, living for 300-500 years and playing host to over 300 other species of wildlife in its lifetime, shedding acorns of its own maturity before returning to the earth whence it came, a continuity of life stimulated by the seasons.

In moist fields and meadows the lovely milkmaids or cuckoo flower, the lady's smock (p.17), is one of the first field flowers to bloom, its pale lilac pink blush colours heralding the farmland spring and the cuckoo's return. Look now for the orange tip butterfly whose foodplant this is, and the small tortoiseshells (p.21), and brimstones now on the wing. The insects of springtime, buzzing and busying along country lanes and hedgerows, speak of sunshine and warmth throughout the land as the various foodplants of their larvae emerge and flower.

There are few wet grasslands in North Devon not graced by the delicately pink lady's smock. As a boy I heard it called laylocks, cuckoo bread, lonesome lady, meadow pink and milk girls. Pick it and 'tis said you will be bitten by an adder (p.91) before the year is out, yet it was used against epilepsy for a while, and in love divination. An old poem refers to it thus:

Tender cress and cuckoo flower:
And curly-haired, fair headed maids,
Sweet was the sound of their singing.

Usually it is pale lilac in colour but sometimes white, and I know places where the flowers are 'doubles', a delightful plant with lonesome lady an apt description for the way it often stands in lonesome fashion at a field edge.

Frogs (p.30) and toads (p.29) have spawned. Soon their tadpoles will be seen in ponds and ditches throughout North Devon, many at traditional sites used for scores of years. Frog spawn is found in large masses, whereas toad spawn is 'necklace' or ribbon-like, found as long strands.

Frogs usually spawn first, as early as January is not uncommon hereabouts, getting later as one moves north from Cornwall up across the UK, as with many seasonal occurrences in nature. Frogs have given their names to a few plants. The saltmarsh glasswort, once called frog grass, was actually used in glass making. Wild arum, commonly called lords and ladies, was also known as frog's meat, whilst frog's foot was a name for the lesser celandine. Early purple orchids were frogs' mouths, a name also given to the monkey flower, *Mimulus luteus*. As for friend toad, the wildflower toadflax is well known and the lovely corn spurrey was called toad's brass in some parts.

Spring woodlands soon ring with birdsong as fresh leaves form a canopy of greenery. The breeding season for many wildlife species is underway. Now more than ever we should keep to footpaths as we wander and enjoy, putting the wildlife first and foremost in our thoughts so as not to disturb and endanger their lives. In April and May the trampling of bluebell leaves, for example, can mean their extinction from a whole area. Even the primrose is the subject of special surveys by Devon County Council as a wildflower in decline despite its apparent abundance as one of our commonest spring flowers.

Springtime woodlands in North Devon have few equals. I grew up in such places soaking up the magic of it all, the birdsong, bluebells (p.36), not carpeted with blue for it is more of a mist, sheer blue enchantment, a time to believe in fairies if ever there was one. It is a plant of Europe's western fringe, rare anywhere else, its old botanical name *Endymion non-scriptus*, but its folk names are crow flower, fairy bells, goosey gander and harebell, the last every bit as magical as the brown hare itself.

Lady's smock or milkmaids, the lovely lonesome lady of wet meadows, was used against epilepsy as well as in love divination, and is also known as the cuckoo flower because it blooms with the coming of the cuckoo.

A powerful glue was once made by scraping bluebell roots, strong enough for gluing the fletching of arrows, or for bookbinding, whilst the bulbs gave a starch second to none. To stand in a bluebell wood amidst the waving flowers and gentle honey scent is to experience springtime with all one's senses.

Cushions of white wood sorrel (p.26) are set amongst their shamrock-like leaves, these once used in a green sauce. Sour grabs we called the plant, and cuckoo cheese, or bird's bread-and-cheese. Fairy bells too, shared with blue-bells. A farmer I knew well called it cuckoo's bread. In some areas it was called 'alleluia' because it blooms at Easter. It gets its names of sleeping beauty or sleeping clover from the folding back of the trifoliate leaves which are every bit as sharply clear as the white flowers.

So with springtime woodlands ringing with birdsong and calls, we can sit beneath a tree to watch and listen as our feathered friends go about their busiest time, the breeding season.

Various bird species including tits, nuthatches and woodpeckers nest in tree holes. The blue or tom tit (p.33) for example may begin laying in nest material at the first signs of spring sunshine, as will great and coal tits though they may delay actual egg laying until they know there will be a plentiful supply of caterpillars and other natural food on which to feed their young.

The nuthatch and treecreeper are usually found in the same habitat type, preferring broadleaved woodland with old trees which provide nest holes and bark crevices, though treecreepers love to roost in certain conifers. The nuthatch is so called from its powerful bill which it uses as a nut-hatchet, often placing nuts in tight crevices to act as a sort of vice.

Treecreepers (p.35) do just that, they creep almost mouse-like up tree trunks in a spiral then fly down to the next tree to begin again. The green wood-pecker (p.34) or yaffle is also known as the rain bird, its far-carrying, almost laughing, call said to be at its loudest and most persistent when rain is imminent. Certainly it sounds clearer at these times.

Many hole-nesting birds will readily take to nestboxes. My photograph shows a female pied flycatcher (p.40) at a nestbox at my private reserve in North Devon, where we have a small 'colony' of up to eight pairs each summer. Pied and spotted flycatchers and common redstarts are all attracted to nestboxes, and as spring and summer migrants which arrive later than many, they find nest-

Dog violets grow and bloom with primroses throughout North Devon, though it is the sweet violet which lends its name to the famous 'Devon Violets' perfume.

boxes a boon when many tree holes are already taken by resident species off to an early start.

For many years I've erected nestboxes, monitoring the results and having some amazing experiences over the course of time. One summer I peeped into a nestbox to find a nuthatch sitting on eggs and the box lid loose. I quickly and gently replaced the lid then placed a heavy rock on top to hold the lid safe, planning to repair it when the nuthatches fledged and left. The following week I went back to check on things and to my amazement the nuthatches had sealed the lid all round with mud and more surprisingly, had then sealed the rock down to the lid! How long this great feat had taken them, and what energy I could only imagine, for the stream with its mud banks was at the bottom of the adjoining field, its meandering taking it away from the bottom of the woods.

As readers will know, nuthatches will take over the old holes of former woodpeckers' nests and using mud will reduce the size to allow only themselves access so they are adept at smooth masonry work. However it was my first experience of box sealing and quite remarkable.

Another incident with nuthatches stays indelibly etched in my memory. I was sitting against a tree watching the adults going in and out of a nestbox with food for their young when I felt a tug at the shoulder of my camouflage shirt. One of the nuthatches had perched briefly on me before flying directly to the nestbox with food. It then continued to use my left shoulder as a perch each time it came from behind en route back home, with me quite transfixed with joy. I have also had treecreepers walk up my legs whilst standing in woodlands and can only suggest to readers, get your outdoor clothing from army surplus stores for close encounters of the bird kind.

The choice of nest sites vary greatly, some nests built into tree forks, others in hedgebanks and behind ivy, and many on or close to the ground. Thus we must take care at this critical time of nests, eggs and young and not trample about willy-nilly in a way that endangers breeding species, be they animal or plant.

Chaffinches (p.41) build very well-camouflaged nests in tree forks, these made using mosses and lichens which blend perfectly with the surrounding habitat. Male wrens build a number of 'cock nests' then the female visits each, eventually choosing one which she will then line and lay her eggs within. These

Nuthatch

little domed nests with their side entrance are cave-like which gives the wren its scientific name *Troglodytes troglodytes*, meaning 'cave dweller'. This is the jenny wren (p.39) of course, and the crackie, names I grew up with in North Devon which remain in use today, crackie no doubt from the bird's lively, loud crackling song, especially when it is scolding us for being too close to its nest. Found in all habitats there's hardly a place in North Devon that one will not find a wren.

As for friend robin, Britain's national bird, it is almost our best friend of the avian world, so used to being with us in our gardens yet it is truly a woodland bird.

Long tailed tits (p.38) do not build in tree holes but make their wonderful 'elastic' nests of mosses held together with cobwebs. Camouflaged with lichens so well, they are difficult to see at all in bramble brakes and suchlike once spring leaves have appeared. The nest is lined with many hundreds of feathers, usually 1200-1500, or even more, an incredibly beautiful construction.

Owls are very much part of the North Devon scene with the tawny owl (p.52, top), also known as the brown or wood owl being the commonest. It is also the screech owl of the 'tu-whit, tu-whoo' calls, and is generally associated with wisdom though the owl of Athene is actually the little owl (p.52, bottom). The 'tu-whit' or sharp 'kee-wick' call is often heard on its own as a hunting tawny flies in the dimmity, or owl light as we call the dusk and dawn times 'yerabouts'. The 'tu-whoo' is often heard as an answering call from its mate.

The little owl is little indeed, being about 8½ inches (21cms) tall and is an introduced species. It is more diurnal, that is a daytime owl, than our other owls and was first brought into Britain by the naturalist Charles Waterton in 1842, as far as we know. Its prey is mainly insects and small mammals. I see the little owl on my travels, often perched on telegraph poles, gate posts and suchlike by day.

Reservoirs are good nature-watching places throughout the year, my own favourite being Wistlandpound (p.45), not far from Blackmoor Gate in North Devon. There is good parking here and a most pleasant walk taking in the open water, woodland and forestry paths. Though dense forestry plantations are sometimes criticised as being poor wildlife habitat the Wistlandpound Reservoir walk never fails to provide good sightings of birds, mammals, insects and wildflowers whenever I visit, and that applies to most reservoirs.

I love, too, the freshwater pools and ditches one comes across in many parts of North Devon, those lovely almost primeval boot-sucking places that actually feel as if they are teeming with wildlife and usually are. Often they are part of wilder streams and rivers, green and buzzing with insect life, the haunt of moorhen, and where mallard breed in springtime.

The moorhen (p.44) is really the mere-hen. In North Devon we call it a dipchick. This sometimes leads to confusion with visiting birdwatchers who know the dabchick or little grebe. Many is the time I've told people of 'lots of dipchicks breeding', which, when they are shown ditches and dykes where 'there's dozens' completely bewilders the uninitiated.

But it is along the faster flowing waterways that we find the much sought-after sightings of kingfisher (p.47) and dipper (p.49), the splashy, chattering streams and rivers which are a common and beautiful feature right across North Devon including Exmoor, and of course on the Taw and Torridge Rivers and their tributaries.

I see kingfishers almost every day downstream of Barnstaple Longbridge, or in the Yeo where it flows into the Taw, and around Pilton Park and beyond. The Torridge, too, is good for them, as is the Caen River and Knowle Water at Braunton, and the lovely Mole at Junction Pool near King's Nympton, the river giving its name to North and South Molton. Look for kingfishers in springtime in their breeding haunts, or in autumn and winter on intertidal waters and estuaries; the halcyon bird, brightly beautiful and, thanks partly to a succession of relatively mild winters, now in good numbers.

The dipper is also known as the water ouzel and water colley, a bird thriving along fresh, faster flowing waterways than the kingfisher. It is rarely seen away from these fast moving waters, with a pair tending to hold about a half mile of territory. It is the only British bird which habitually walks and 'flies' underwater, a remarkable sight as it hunts for food which comprises mainly beetles and insect larvae. Colley means 'dark as coal', no doubt from the dark slatey grey and chocolate brown plumage which contrasts greatly with the dazzling white breast. The name dipper describes well its constant dipping and bobbing movements as it perches on rocks along a waterway.

Wherever we find dippers there will we also see the grey wagtails, another dipping and bobbing species, a trait definitely linked with moving water habitats and seen also in some wading birds, I think to help camouflage them at breed-

The small tortoiseshell, once a common butterfly yet declining in recent years. One hopes for a rapid recovery of this and other butterflies for if not, then nature conservation is not working too well.

ing haunts. One summer after heavy rains and flooding, which caused the destruction of a grey wagtail nest and young, I observed the wagtails helping to feed the young of dippers which had survived the flooding. The parent dippers were obviously quite happy with this situation; a summer never to be forgotten.

But let's look at some of our animals, never so easily observed as birds, but sitting quietly in subdued 'country' colours does mean we'll see far more than might be imagined.

In April or May fox cubs will be seen near their earths as they romp and play-fight in the learning games of their kind. Dog foxes occasionally help with the early teaching of the cubs on evening hunting forays, the cubs remaining with the vixen usually into late summer or early autumn, when they disperse to find their own patch. Foxes are common in North Devon with some subject to the mange as I write this, a contagious disease most notable in the loss of the animal's coat.

Grey squirrels are common in North Devon and holding a stable population which fluctuates from time to time in some areas. There was a relict population of red squirrels for a while into the 1970s and signs of some about at present which may be due to unpublicised releases. Grey squirrels do not hibernate as is sometimes thought. According to a widespread European superstition it is extremely unlucky to kill a squirrel. It is said that the animal hid its eyes with its tail when it saw Adam and Eve eating the forbidden fruit in the Garden of Eden and thus acquired the bushy tail it now has. Anyone who kills a squirrel will, it is said, henceforth lose all hunting skills.

The Mustelldae family is well represented in the area with stoats (p.51), weasels (p.50), otters and badgers all native, and the mink which is now feral, that is breeding in the wild following escapes and releases from captive fur farms since the 1950s.

Though stoats are larger than weasels the chances of seeing both together is very unlikely, thus the best way to tell them apart is that stoats have black tipped tails whereas weasels do not. Both are fierce little hunters and interesting to observe. Weasels in particular tend to be very curious so if you see one dive into a hole or some other cover, stay about and it will almost certainly appear again to have a look at the strange creature trying to observe it.

A chiff-chaff feeding its young at a nest site which is always on or close to the ground. All the more reason to keep strictly to footpaths, particularly during spring and summer when such creatures are breeding and extremely vulnerable.

The lovely River Torridge in 'Tarka Country', the scene as we look downstream from Canal Bridge to the former rail bridge, now part of the Tarka Trail, between Bideford and Torrington. This is North Devon farming country at its loveliest.

Beam Weir, near Canal Bridge. Close to Torrington this lovely weir is the home of otters, herons and other wildlife and is easily viewed from the Tarka Trail near the Puffing Billy Restaurant. Salmon and trout can be watched here.

Wood Sorrel. The wild woodland oxalis also known as bird's bread-and-cheese, its leaves can be eaten as a green sauce. This is one of the 'shamrocks' of Ireland and the sour sabs (crabs) of Devon.

A grey wagtail feeds her young in a nest hidden in a riverbank crevice. Such sites are vulnerable so please tread carefully. A common resident species in North Devon, along most waterways.

*A young oak shoot raises above the ground where it may live for 300–500 years
and host over 300 other wildlife species as provider of food and shelter.*

The magical toad will actually befriend the gardener. One would come to my call each evening as dusk approached. Prone to road kills there are several 'Toad Crossing' patrols in North Devon.

From the shelter of a pond a frog gazes at the camera, asking only to be left some watery habitat and a bit of peace and seclusion.

Reflections in a woodland pool. One of the best places to observe wildlife is a wood edge with water about.

Spring woods. Where better to wander to listen to bird song and breathe in the essence of the North Devon countryside?

A blue tit brings food to its young in a natural nest hole, timing egg-laying to fit with, hopefully, an abundance of caterpillars and other insects with which to feed its young.

Green woodpeckers nest in tree holes which they hack out of the bole, an amazing feat. This is the yaffle, rain-bird or miller's advisor.

Treecreepers nest behind bark crevices and, like the nuthatch, are found in North Devon's broadleaved woodlands.

Bluebells, a mist of blue rising over the woodland floor in April and May, one of the loveliest sights of a North Devon springtime.

A female blackbird on her nest. She is one of the earliest songbirds to breed, often raising two or three broods each year.

Long tailed tits feeding young. The wonderful 'elastic' nest may contain well over 1000 feathers in the lining.

Male wrens build two or three 'cock nests' then the female makes her choice and lines the one she decides will be home for eggs and young.

A female pied flycatcher at its nestbox. The numbering indicates a sequence in a particular nestbox scheme for ease of monitoring.

Chaffinches build neat nests, often in tree forks, camouflaging them so well they are extremely difficult to distinguish from the surrounding bark and foliage.

Skylark young, mouths gaping for food. This species nests on the ground so is particularly vulnerable to weather, predation and our wandering in the countryside.

A dunnock feeds a young cuckoo. Dunnocks, meadow pipits and reed warblers are common host species of cuckoos, although the cuckoo itself is now in serious decline.

A moorhen wandering its wetland habitat in that peculiar jerky motion they have. This is the dipchick of Devon, a common local name. It was formerly known as the mere-hen, for it is a bird of meres rather than moors.

Wistlandpound Reservoir lies near Blackmoor Gate, a glorious place for nature-watching at any time of year.

River and stream wildlife. Some of my favourite haunts are the waterways of North Devon, magical places which are also the homes of otter, salmon and dragonflies galore.

Kingfisher perching near its riverbank home; such splendid colour and power in a tiny bird. It is doing well generally in North Devon these days due in part to a succession of mild winters.

Grey herons, here at a favourite fishing pool, are so much a part of our rivers, streams, lakes and marshes. There is an ancient heronry at the National Trust property, Arlington Court, visible from the lake area.

The dipper, emblem of the Devon Wildlife Trust and a territorial bird of swift flowing waterways such as the lovely Lyn River, which gives its name both to Lynton and Lynmouth.

Weasels are tiny but fierce predators and one of the Mustelldae family which includes stoats, otters and badgers, all part of North Devon's fascinating fauna.

Stoats are larger than weasels and always have black tipped tails, a useful identification guide. They may often be seen hunting around dusk and dawn. Ermine is the white winter coat of the stoat.

Two owl studies. A sleepy tawny owl (left) and the much smaller little owl; the latter being more evident during daylight hours.

A young fox explores its woodland home where it feeds on small mammals and even blackberries and fungi, as well as carrion. Cubs are born in the spring and may be seen about with the vixen on evenings well into the summer.

Buttercups

Summer

Viper's bugloss and wallpepper or yellow stonecrop. These two brightly beautiful wildflowers are part of our coastal flora and may be found at Braunton Burrows in the summer months, along with the evening primrose and various orchids, thriving amongst the dunes and wet slacks.

It is summertime and we are on the Torridge River twixt Bideford and Great Torrington, standing on Canal Bridge looking down to the former rail bridge now part of the Tarka Trail. The trail and indeed Tarka Country, is named after Henry Williamson's *Tarka the Otter* – a classic country tale of an otter's life – the trail taking in some 180 miles followed by Tarka during his lifetime. Williamson's Tarka was taken as a tourism hook, a Devon County Council initiative along the lines of Dorset's Hardy Country, and now is big business almost 80 years after the story was first written and published. Tarka was born here by Beam Weir and Canal Bridge (p.74), the latter once carrying an aqueduct across the river hence its name. Otters still live here and on the other rivers of North Devon, the West Country a stronghold for the species now subject to special conservation measures as an endangered species since the 1970s.

Beam Weir is set amidst attractive farmland, the Torridge here teeming with widlife including grey herons which may be observed from the Tarka Trail fishing along the weir, or downstream. There is a heronry (p.48) not far away at Annery, near the pretty village of Weare Gifford.

It is still a rare pleasure to see an otter (p.75) in the wild, mainly because they have a largely nocturnal lifestyle, avoiding human presence wherever possible. Thus we are more likely to see their tracks and signs, usually the five-toed footprints in the mud. They also mark territory with their droppings, called spraints, but these are small and not easy to find.

Otters may have cubs at any time of the year though in my experience most are born in the spring or early summer. They usually stay with the mother or bitch otter for the first nine or ten months then move on to find territories of their own.

Canal Bridge is best viewed from the Tarka Trail and with Beam Weir can easily be reached by walking downstream from the Puffing Billy Restaurant near Torrington. Other Tarka landmarks hereabouts include the claypits at Merton, the Trail going by this village and on to Meeth, and to Bideford and Barnstaple in the other direction.

Also in the Torridge District, but on the coast, is the famous traffic-free village of Clovelly, well worth a visit for its own sake though from a wildlife point of view visit it from the Hobby Drive, a superb walk, well wooded and with fine coastal views along its length.

For me some of the best summer nature-watching is to be found at dawn and dusk, with woodland edges across the whole of North Devon providing some of the best sightings. Thus we are well served, for wherever we live or are staying there are woodlands to be found close at hand, binoculars and a bin liner to sit on being all the equipment one needs to enjoy a day in the countryside. Look more closely about you, at the sunlight through the leaves of the trees perhaps, or at the various lichens (p.85) on trees or stones. A good crop of lichens is a sign of a healthy unpolluted atmosphere 'tis said, so with an abundance of lichens about we should be healthily well off in North Devon.

I still find it odd that so many people who love to see butterflies about tend to give moths a somewhat half-hearted appraisal. It must be partly to do with moths being largely nocturnal, yet they are often as brightly coloured and beautifully patterned as any butterfly.

The photograph of an angle shades moth (p.83) clearly shows just how beautiful these insects can be. Angle shades may be found in all seasons of the year but in North Devon are most common from May to September. Its caterpillars feed mainly on groundsel, bracken and dock, but will take most herbaceous plants. When resting on herbage or tree trunks they look very like leaves. There are numerous day-flying moths.

Now in summertime sparrowhawks either have eggs or young in loosely built platform nests made of twigs broken off with the beak. These small hawks will nest in conifers or broadleaved trees, usually laying from May to July. They are solitary nesters usually though I once found two occupied nests, in dense woodland, only 30 yards apart in adjoining trees. Monitoring these for the British Trust for Ornithology Nest Record Scheme I discovered it was the second closest nesting record ever, with two nests in a Dumfriesshire woodland being the closest ever recorded at a distance of 22 yards.

Female sparrowhawks are wonderful mothers and the photograph (p.88) shows a female sheltering her downy young in pouring rain in what was a mixed summer of heat waves and rainstorms. The following week she was perched on the nest edge in absolutely blazing sunshine, wings open to throw a cooling shadow on her young. Indeed as the day progressed and the sun moved across the sky so she moved around the nest edge to maintain the cooling situation as best she could. Quite wonderful.

A rabbit watches the day from a sandy burrow near the coast. Rabbits are fairly common again since myxomatosis decimated the population in the 1950s. The disease is now enzootic with occasional outbreaks occurring throughout North Devon.

The buzzard (p.89) is probably the best known bird of prey in North Devon, commonly seen soaring in circles over woods and farmland with splayed wing tips, crying the piercing, mewing call we all know so well. With a wingspan of up to four feet they are splendid birds, taking rats, rabbits and other mammals as prey, as well as beetles and such, and carrion. Once when nest monitoring I peered into a buzzard's nest and found an adder staring at me but it was dead, though I am sure I climbed down from that tree in record time just in case!

I've found buzzards nesting in trees mostly but also in cliffs, in small caves and in quarries where tree trunks grow out from quarry faces. They lay usually from April to June so may have young in the nest into August in some years. Incubation is about 35 days, with fledging around 45 days so it is a fairly long breeding season with only one brood per year.

The sight of a barn owl launching from a tree sends a thrill of excitement through me and fortunately, though a bird in decline, there are barn owls spread, albeit less commonly these days, across North Devon. Barn owls are also known as screech owls and anyone who has heard their hunting calls at night in lonely places will have no doubt how some ghost stories came about, especially when the white shape and silent flight adds to the haunting atmosphere. Of great benefit to mankind, the barn owl kills rats and other vermin associated with farming yet it was also thought of as a creature of doom and death by misguided folk not so long ago. But not so, a fabulous bird the barn owl.

They actually have a very long breeding season especially for a bird which may well raise two broods in a year. Incubation by the female takes about 34 days, with fledging from 9 to 12 weeks. Now that's four months all told, a long time indeed if two broods are raised.

Summer on Exmoor, and one-third of Exmoor's National Park is in North Devon, is a wonderful time for nature-watching. It is my favourite time for the moor. Though I would agree 'fair weather' naturalists don't know what they are missing half the time, there is no doubt that a secluded Exmoor combe on a sunny day in summer brings more wildlife to our notice. Even during the height of the tourist season it is possible to get far away from the madding crowd to find peace and solitude, which is why I love honeypot areas so much. I go somewhere else.

Challacombe and its environs is one of many such places, a pleasant little village, a friendly inn and fine walks. I love the walk from Breakneck Hole car park. Just along the road uphill away from Challacombe on the left is a gateway and stile to Wood Barrow. Along this route we pass the Bill Hill and Edgerly standing stones, then up over the moor over fairly rugged terrain to follow stone walls and wind-shaped hawthorns to Wood Barrow Gate and the Wood Barrow itself. Walks are signposted to Pinkworthy (or Pinkery) Pond too, but I go on via cotton grass country to seek out the magnificent Longstone menhir which at 9ft tall is the most imposing of its kind on Exmoor. Then, in over amongst the rushes and sedges to a trickle of water which is the Bray River and follow this on down a sun-happy combe for a picnic in a little beech wood which hides the remains of an old farm. There are always redstarts hereabouts and whinchats, with stonechats (p.92) further down the combe as, picnic over, we head for Swincombe or Challacombe Reservoir. Red deer are often met with here and foxes (p.53) in broad daylight as ravens fly overhead and swallows dip in the calm waters of the reservoir itself. This is one of my favourite walks and that of Bracken my border collie, friend and companion, who loved these wild places as I do.

And where can be better than the Exmoor combes with their swift flowing waterways, sheep running wild and hardy, as dippers and ring ouzels feed young and tell of the time of year better than any calendar. Here we meet with the various dragonflies and damselflies, the so-called devil's darning needles or horse stingers that neither bite us nor do they sting.

Amazing isn't it that these insects whose ancestors saw the time of dinosaurs, live but a few weeks in which to mate, lay eggs and set down the future of their kind. But prior to their emergence as flying insects their nymphs have wandered submerged beneath the waters for between two to five years feeding voraciously until nature's signal tells them to climb some bankside vegetation, split open and release the beautiful winged insect into the world.

My photo shows the golden-ringed dragonfly (p.79), a busy and graceful insect some 74mm or so in length. They cruise low along the waterways showing amazing manoeuvrability and are often found with beautiful demoiselle and large red damselflies. If you see one patrolling a waterway wait in one spot for it will pass by repeatedly. To think that 250 million years ago the first true dragonflies zoomed about and here we are today able to enjoy their iridescent beauty as they fly, flutter and flicker in the sunlight – 'ansome.

A cow gazes from charlock as we wander North Devon's beautiful farming country in summer, but please remember the Country Code, keeping to footpaths and closing gates etc.

And so to the more farmed areas of North Devon, with their own mix of nat-ural and man-made beauty, much of the area retaining the patchwork of fields with hedgerows. Much has been lost it is true but there are signs of a return to traditional farming which was not so long ago the very essence of North Devon: people, the land and nature getting along together.

As I write this I am conscious of the unease in the countryside. At the begin-ning of the new millennium, the twenty-first century, there was a euphoria that sadly lasted only about 'five minutes', so to speak, as the whole nation was then swept up in the tragic foot and mouth disease crisis. It was a farming matter but not just about farming, it was about all people and animals and just about everything really, our whole environment, aching as it were beneath the sad weight of the moment.

And thus I feel sheep in the landscape and a cow (p.60) in a blaze of golden flowered *cruciferae* epitomise the very essence of North Devon and its farming community, all of us who eat, for it is the farmer who feeds us and our chil-dren. I loved the scene created by chickens (p.63) free ranging it in a large grassy run, and hope by the time this book is published all is well and healed in the countryside once more.

Occasionally I am asked why I am so devoted to wildlife and to nature. Really it's what I know best. Perhaps against other things it could be weighed as all I know, right from earliest boyhood days. That's another story but it is the answer to the question, and having gained so much from the wildlife of the countryside, from nature, it is right to give back, to put back if one is able.

So let us look at one or two butterflies, a grassland species and a woodland species, the marbled white and the silver washed fritillary respectively, and find out how interesting they are.

The marbled white is the only British butterfly with the distinctive black and white pattern and in the early nineteenth century it was known as the half-mourner. This name came from the black and white dresses worn by women in half mourning when only black was worn in full mourning. The name then changed to the marmoris and marmoress, from the word marmoreal which means 'like marble'. Later in the nineteenth century the butterfly finally became known as the marbled white. It is actually a black butterfly with white spots, with the patterning sometimes varying considerably, and it is a member of the brown family, not one of the whites.

Tranquillity itself: sheep in pasture shaded by trees, North Devon at its loveliest.

Like the ringlet the marbled white lays its eggs while in flight over grasses such as sheep's fescue and cocksfoot which are foodplants for its caterpillars or larvae. The scientific name *Melanargia galathea* also speaks of the colouring, with 'melan', black and 'arges', white. Galatea was a nymph beloved by Polyphemus, the name given by Linnaeus. Look for this charming butterfly from July into August.

The silver-washed fritillary has a wash of silver suffusing its underwings and is a large stunningly beautiful orange-winged insect with dark patterning. It is the largest British fritillary and may be seen in sunlit woodlands where it roosts in the trees by night, flying in July and August. The butterfly is unique in Britain in laying its eggs on tree trunks, favouring oak trees where its foodplant the violet is growing. The caterpillar hibernates on the tree trunk until springtime when it descends to feed on violet leaves.

One of my favourite places to watch these, in sun dappled woods as wood warblers and pied flycatchers call, is along the lovely Badgworthy (or Badgery) Water near Malmsmead. Magic!

Another of my favourite insects is the green lacewing (p.82), my favourite colour being green. The transluscent wings of this delicate insect give a fairy-like appearance, as do the fascinating large golden eyes which glow like embers when they catch the sunlight.

The summer generation of these lovely insects is produced from a spring generation which has emerged from winter hibernation. The summer generation then produces the next generation which hibernates through the winter, and so on. Usually found low down on vegetation the green lacewing rarely flies by day but what a fine insect it is.

And what is summer without the call of the cuckoo, a bird so common when I was a boy that it was heard in every valley in North Devon all spring and summer. Today it is, like so many other species, in decline, and one stops to listen to its evocative call, rather than miss it. Various birds play host to the cuckoo, with notably the reed warbler, meadow pipit and dunnock (p.43) among these. It is interesting that cuckoos, which regularly target a particular host species, lay eggs which closely resemble the colouring of the eggs of that species.

As a migratory bird which arrives with us in April, it lends its name to several spring flowers including cuckoo flower for lady's smock and ragged robin, cuckoo pint to the wild arum we also know as lords and ladies and snakefood. Cuckoo spit, the frothy protection for young froghopper bugs seen on various plants is another name-only link with this bird, whilst as long ago as the thirteenth century the following rhyme was written to come down through the centuries to the present day.

Summer is icumen in
Lludg sing cuccu
Spryngeth sed and bloweth mede
And groweth the wude nu.

And

In April come he will,
In May he sings all day,
In June he changes tune,
In July he prepares to fly,
In August go he must.

Today we know the cuckoo flies back to Africa for what is our winter, yet not so long ago it was thought it hibernated in tree stumps, whilst another belief was that it changed into a hawk. This latter belief is not so surprising when one considers the similarity twixt cuckoo and sparrowhawk when observed in hedge-hopping flight across the countryside.

I do a lot of badger watching in high summer, getting into a favourite spot before sunset to watch these wonderful animals about their business of foraging for food, or in play with cubs about, or maybe changing their bedding, for they are clean animals and great characters of ancient origin (p.77). Badgers are present in many a North Devon wooded valley and may be seen about by day in more secluded places if one is very fortunate. The typical badger is a grey animal in appearance with a black and white striped head. However, there are sometimes considerable variations in hair colour with at least three very recognisable colour variations, melanistic, albino and erythristic, with intermediates between these. Here in North Devon I have seen very dark, almost black, badgers, cream-coloured badgers and quite reddish ones, the erythristic, which can look almost ginger. This is not due to the soil colouring though in some areas such as Brendon in Somerset, red soil will discolour the normal hair colouring.

Free ranging chickens are always a fine sight.

The warm scent of the summer blossoms of guelder rose (p.73) fills the air at times on fine evenings, this small tree a delight in many a hedgerow. There is a pleasing, hopeful continuity about the blossom and then the fruit of such trees and shrubs, as we all surely feel when the flowers of bramble turn to become blackberries. The tree, some call it a shrub, grows well in the oak woods and damp hedgerow areas across North Devon and has maple-like leaves. An old name is swamp or water elder which tells of its liking for wet habitats where it thrives along with alder and willow. Look carefully at the blossoms and you will see small fertile flowers surrounded by larger, showy infertile flowers, these attracting insects to those further in. The guelder roses I have growing with us at my private reserve are handsome trees, 20 feet or so in height.

In North Devon I always liken the primroses and bluebells to spring and the superb up-thrusting foxglove (p.78) to summer, for as the days show more sunshine so this fairly common wildflower is suddenly in bloom and as cheerful as the day is long. The oval or lance-shaped leaves tell of the flowers to come as early as March, and then from June to August the hedgerows and wood edges are lit purple by the 'fairy bells' beloved of bees and other insects. There may be from 20 to 80 flowers on a single stem which always hang at the top and on one side. This is the wild flower that yields the drug digitalis, used in the treatment of heart complaints. Like so many of our wild plants, it is a friend in real terms for its medicinal value as well as its beauty.

And what is summertime in North Devon without fields of buttercups? One of the traditional sights of the countryside despite the increased use of weed-killers, a buttercup meadow in sunshine is quite breathtakingly beautiful, the flowers reaching to 3ft tall and majestic (p.54). Even today children hold a meadow buttercup flower beneath each other's chins to see if they like butter.

Thrift, also known as sea pink.

It was thought that the roots ground up with salt cured the plague, and that hung around the neck in a bag the flowers cured lunacy. The meadow buttercup is the commonest and best known of our three most common species, the other two being bulbous and creeping. In the bulbous, the base of the stem is swollen and each leaf has a stalked middle lobe. The sepals are bent back. As its name suggests, the creeping buttercup is a wide-spreading plant with creeping runners.

Sunlight catches the shining web of a common garden or orb spider, the spider sitting in the centre waiting for an insect to become caught in the sticky drops on the spiral thread. Britain has over 600 species of spiders, all of them harmless to us. They are not insects but arachnids and have eight legs, not six as all insects have. The word insect, by the way, is short for in-sections, referring to the head, thorax and abdomen of these amazing and varied creatures.

Around the coast of North Devon are a few sand dune systems such as those at Northam Country Park, Instow, Braunton Burrows (p.66), Saunton and Croyde. They form part of the beaches which attract so many visitors to the area during the summer, tourism being a huge source income to North Devon.

But these dune systems are also very important to wildlife with some rare species of flora at places such as Braunton Burrows, along with more common, strikingly beautiful plants such as evening primrose and viper's bugloss which are at their best from around June to August.

The evening primrose loves dunes and waste places and is a tall plant with glorious yellow flowers. It is an annual herb with a large fleshy rootstock once used as a vegetable. It is more closely related to the willow herb than the primrose family and is attractive to insects, including moths. An oil prepared from evening primroses is being used increasingly for treating hyperactivity in children, and other nervous disorders. The oil is used in cosmetics, skin lotions and to alleviate discomfort in women at pre-menstrual times; the seeds were chewed by Native American women for the very same purpose.

It is wonderful is it not, to walk amongst beautiful wildflowers knowing also of their benefits to human kind, to think back to one's school days and remember voices lifted to the words 'All things bright and beautiful' echoing from a school building.

And viper's bugloss, what a strange English name for a wildflower, seen in my photo (p.56) growing with wall pepper on the dunes. The name derives from a belief that the plant could be used to cure snake bites, the seeds also used in a drink to cure melancholy. This is the common viper's bugloss which grows 3ft tall and is a beautiful blue-purple colour when in full flower, and which is a member of the borage family. The nutlet-like seeds in autumn resemble a viper's head which is another reason for its English name. Bees, butterflies and other insects visit the flowers for nectar.

The brightly golden stonecrop is *Sedum acre*, acre meaning bitter which gives its other English names, wall pepper and biting stonecrop, referring to the peppery taste of its tiny leaves.

All such flowers of a North Devon summer and its wild places are still unspoiled by the march of progress and let's hope they will remain so as more and more people come to realise and appreciate that being close to nature is a very good thing indeed.

Walk any rich farmland area, or the sandy dunes and coast and we will find rabbits (p.58), some now doing well again despite the ravages of myxomatosis spread in the 1950s. Introduced from France in the twelfth century the rabbit was highly valued for its meat and protected by landowners for hundreds of years, with poaching severely punished. How times change! A social animal the rabbit lives in colonies in warrens, the below-ground tunnels or burrows interconnected. Best looked for at feeding time, at dawn or dusk, rabbits are interesting to watch. Getting to know a warren and its inhabitants makes for an interesting study.

Inland from Braunton Burrows is a large expanse of marshland (p.71) grazed by cattle and sheep and having a fascinating flora and fauna. I prefer it to the Burrows myself, loving the open expanses of greenness, and the hand-dug dykes made in the nineteenth century and now maintained by machinery, a marvellous piece of history and heritage. This is an area truly rich in wildlife and particularly good for *odonata* species, the dragonflies and damselflies that rely so much on these habitats. The mute swans (p.76) which may be seen on the estuary during the autumn and winter will be here with young now, the grey downy cygnets we all love to see with their devoted parents. Cobs and pens are the adult males and females respectively, powerful birds well known by their almost honking wingbeats when in flight. I have seen cobs put many a fox to flight when the hunter has moved too close to the cygnets, and many a person, too, come to that. There are few creatures more graceful than a mute swan on the water. Grace and power, that is the mute swan.

Pairs mate for life, building an enormous nest of reeds and other aquatic plants, collected by the male who gives them to the female who then builds the nest. From 5–8 eggs are laid, usually from late April into May, these are incubated by the female for 35–56 days whilst the male mounts guard nearby, a bird fearless in defence of nest and young.

In nearby grasslands away from the water and even in the dune slacks,

The flower-rich dunes of Braunton Burrows are best visited from June to August for their floral interest.

skylarks will be nesting (p.42). It is almost beyond belief that this species once so common, even just a few years ago, is now in such serious decline that some conservation organisations are saying the bird could become extinct in the UK in a very few years. Part of its problem is in the vulnerability of its nest sites on the ground.

Everyone thinks of a skylark as singing high in the sky on rapidly beating wings, such a safe place, but somewhere below concealed by grasses or some crop will be a nest with eggs or young. If eggs, then they will be incubated by the female for about 11 days. If young, both parents will feed them for about 10 days in the nest and, subsequently, nearby until they become fully fledged after some 20 days. With luck two clutches are laid each year and with a lot of luck the young may survive to adulthood. Changes in farming practice, people pressure, bad weather, pesticides, predation, all take their toll and the tiny lark is now a threatened species.

I found a skylark singing

I'm not too sure I understand,
What has happened to our land,
My parents say skylarks were everywhere,
Even when I was born, yet I am only fourteen,
So where did they go? Where? Into thin air?
I'm not sure I understand.

My father says when he was a child,
More land was clean, more land was wild,
That skylark sound was loud upon the air,
That wildlife, all kinds, was everywhere,
That the countryside was good, not defiled,
My father says when he was a child.

Yesterday I found a skylark singing,
As above my head I watched it winging,
A speck of whirring wings in a clear blue sky,
Even its song was whirring from on high,
Somewhere close by four or five eggs are lying,
That means soon as many skylarks flying.

*Exmoor's wildest combes are superb wildlife habitats with many surviving thanks
to landowners and the Exmoor National Park Authority in partnership.*

I think we'll win and skylarks will survive,
I think I know this lovely bird will thrive,
That I will know skylarks are everywhere,
Because in knowing the truth people will care,
I can't believe the skylark that I see
Could one day just be part of history.

My thanks to my son, Robin, for the above poem which won the *BBC Wildlife Magazine's* Young Poet of the Year Award recently.

It seems rather odd when one looks around at so much open countryside, that any creature or plant should become endangered yet many are. As we walk the wide open spaces along say, the banks of a river on a sunny day with perhaps a sailing boat or two skimming the waters, all seems well. Yet today where I sit watching the river near my home, listening to the song of a skylark, just five years ago I noted a dozen in my diary. When I was a lad the sky over my home was filled with bats, and conservation had not been invented. Today when I see bats flitting about on a dimmity summer's eve I stop and stare and wonder whether I'll see them here at all in a few years' time. And this is still very rural North Devon!

But life goes on, the summer bringing locals out and about to the beautiful coast to mix with visitors from all over. Grockles we'd say, yet grockles we become ourselves as we set off on our holidays.

Stand overlooking Ilfracombe Harbour in July or August when family holidaymakers are here, the children loving the beaches and ice creams, and who would deny them jolly times. See them playing at Watermouth, Woolacombe or Westward Ho! Stand by the rock pools at Croyde's Downend where acres of beach remain free of people who tend to crowd into certain areas as gregarious as house sparrows.

Wander up to Baggy Point, passing happy people coming the other way then sit gazing and lazing as seabirds clamour above waves breaking on rugged rocks below their breeding cliffs.

At Lee Bay (p.100) I watched my collie, Bracken, search for stones as the surf chased him in and he turned and chased the receding waves back out again.

Walk to the sound of chakking stonechat families calling from scented gorse in the Valley of Rocks as swallows, martins and swifts scream after highflying insects overhead, and painted lady butterflies come flying around the coast with a few clouded yellows. We sit where Samuel Palmer, the landscape artist, probably sat on a great flat rock overlooking the sea.

Wringcliff Bay is down below, people sunbathing looking like ants in the distance. I follow Jan Ridd's footsteps, he of *Lorna Doone*, up to Mother Meldrum's Kitchen and the Cheesewring. It's as well Jan married Lorna Doone for to have traipsed all this way from his Exmoor home and then not to have wed her would hardly have been worth the trip. Still, he'd have enjoyed the superb scenery here westwards from what is now Lee Abbey (p.101), and on to Woody Bay (p.99) and Heddon's Mouth, and the wildlife too. R.D. Blackmore must certainly have appreciated it.

The heady scent of gorse (p.94) fills our senses, along with its colour. We can stand, stare and feel the luxuriance, the zest for life the plant has, as if it remembers past times when it was needed by us as fodder for wintering livestock and fuel for our ovens, as well as for its golden and green beauty. Gorse and buttercup days are summer days yet gorse may flower to cheer us throughout the year. An old saying goes, 'when gorse is out of flower kissing is out of season', and here in North Devon there obviously is no lack of either. And what a fine summery wine the flowers make, and if one feels a tad unsteady afterwards there are few better walking sticks than those made from a stout, straight stem of gorse.

Gorse is the furze or fuzz put over a doorway to ward off bad spirits, and the whin which gives the little whinchat its name. There is a dwarf or western gorse also to be found on coast or moorland, beautiful when mixed with heather and tough on the socks and trousers of walkers.

Pink thrift graces our clifftops too, nodding in the sea breezes, thriving in saltmarshes, also on some pasture land (p.64). Often called sea pink it is a popular garden plant valued for its beauty, and some may remember it as the plant on the reverse of the old twelve-sided threepenny bits. Look closely at this lovely plant and you will see the flowers are grouped into dense hemispherical heads, the 'flower' the eye first sees actually being a cluster of many. Old names include ladies' cushion and the Gaelic *tonn a cladaich*, or 'beach wave'. 'ansome!

Amongst the pink thrift new life explores a North Devon clifftop. Downy

A scene of glorious wildflowers across Braunton Marshes. This is high grade grazing land and important also for wildlife.

with grey and dark blotches, the little herring gull chick (p.104) pecks away at the stony soil near the scrape of a nest lined by its parents. The adult female gull laid just the one egg this year then she and her mate incubated it for 32 days until it hatched. Now both parents will look after the chick until it fledges at around 6 weeks; the whole colony here busy about their nesting and raising of young ones.

Their strange laughing call gives them local names of cat gull and white maa. Impressive birds and great fliers they are so much part and parcel of the seaside scene.

The North Devon coast has, in fact, some fine seabird habitat, with razorbills (p.107) and guillemots (p103), the two common members of the auk family, along with puffins nesting on the island of Lundy some eleven miles out to sea. And there are kittiwakes (p105) too, the gentlest looking of all the gulls, so named from their calls, a haunting sort of 'kitti-kitti-wake' ringing from their cliff-ledge colonies during courtship and nesting times. They are very much maritime gulls, coming to land just as far as the coastal cliffs during this summer breeding time. An old belief is that the souls of dead children become kittiwakes, a charming belief probably brought about by the gentle expression and haunting cries of these delightful gulls.

Living by a tidal river where I walk each day to nature-watch, I see the thousands of waders along with wildfowl during autumn and winter. One species that always catches the eye is the oystercatcher, its pied plumage and long orange bill and legs making it an easy bird to identify. What isn't always realised is that some oystercatchers remain to breed on the North Devon coast amongst the summer wildflowers on clifftop grass sward.

Sea pie they were once called, and mussel picker, both names probably more accurate than oystercatcher for it is unlikely our British birds encounter oysters to any extent, though to watch them using their powerful orange bills to prise limpets and mussels is quite an experience.

I have sat at a distance many times watching oystercatchers (p.106) on the sea cliffs at nesting time. A large scrape is the nest, often unlined though I have seen both adults use small pebbles, shells and sometimes thrift flowers as a scant lining. They usually nest in solitary fashion though in a favourable habitat we may find them near together. I have also seen two females lay in the same scrape at times. Incubation takes about 27 days from when the last egg is laid, with young staying in the nest for a couple of days then wandering about with their parents and fledging fully at about 5 weeks. It is a treat to watch a mother oystercatcher wander the tideline of a quiet cove with her youngsters in tow.

A sound like two stones being struck together in these same coastal habitats, or perhaps in dune country or on the moors, is quite likely to be the call of a stonechat. My photo (p.92) shows a male resplendent with velvety black head, white collar and chestnut orange breast, a rather striking bird. Females are more quietly coloured but just as lovely, the difference being that he has to show up whilst holding territory in the breeding season, while she, like many other species with less colourful plumage, needs to be better camouflaged on the nest. It is a fascinating world, the world of nature.

Female stonechats build the nest as well as dealing with the incubation of the eggs for two weeks. Fledging, with both adults feeding the young, takes about 14–16 days. Two broods are not uncommon in North Devon and I have known three. As with many a bird species the nests may be at ground level and thus extremely vulnerable to our traipsing around.

Want to photograph a stonechat? A useful tip is to bang two stones together in the vicinity of a known territory. The cockbird will be most put out that another 'male' is about and will show himself on top of some nearby shrub, calling away in a 'who goes there?' fashion. Take your pictures then leave so that the birds can get on with the task of sorting out the next generation of stonechats in peace.

The buzzing of bees around the same gorse brake where the stonechat calls to his newly fledged family takes us on into the autumn of the year. The breeding season as we think of it has ended and leaves begin to turn colour, borrowing gold from the gorse flower, and reddish orange from the bills of oystercatchers, as swallows twitter and gather for the great journey back to their winter quarters…

Guelder rose blossom. Note the smaller fertile flowers within the circle of large infertile flowers, which guide the insects in to pollinate.

Canal Bridge on the River Torridge between Bideford and Torrington. A heron fishes in the foreground, perhaps a descendant of Old Nog the grey heron of Williamson's Tarka the Otter.

Mother and cub otters at sunset. Otters hold a stable population in North Devon but we are more likely to see their footprints, called seals, in the mud of river-banks, as the otter is a shy creature as well as being mainly nocturnal.

Typical tree root system otter bolt.

A mute swan with cygnets along the dyke at Braunton Marshes, a place rich in bankside vegetation, birds and insect life. Good for nature-watching all year round.

Badgers out and about in the North Devon countryside, creatures of ancient origin related to otters, stoats and weasels.

Foxgloves, the lovely fairy bells of summertime, source of digitalis used to help heart conditions.

A golden-ringed dragonfly perches in the warmth of the sun. Watch for these insects patrolling waterways as they hawk for smaller insects as food.

Marbled white butterflies, once known as half mourners, a butterfly of summer grasslands in July and August.

Silver-washed fritillary, a butterfly of summer woodlands where violets can be found as its caterpillar foodplant.

A green lacewing perches low on riverbank foliage, a most beautiful insect not uncommon in North Devon.

An angle shades moth, mainly on the wing from May-September, its caterpillars feeding on groundsel, bracken and dock.

Sunshine through sycamore leaves, such simple scenes of summer beauty make good photographs.

Lichens are a sign of an unpolluted environment it is said.

A barn owl launches from a tree branch perch, its ghostly white silent shape and weird shrieks probably the origin of many a haunting tale. Despite worrying declines there are still quite a few about in North Devon.

Barn owl young. Serious declines in this species have resulted in special measures to ensure its protection. Barn owls take readily to nestboxes and their future is one of hope.

Soaked by summer rainstorms, a female sparrowhawk shelters her downy young from the worst of the weather. Afforestation has helped the species increase in North Devon.

A buzzard perches on a woodland tree stump, perhaps our best known raptor and a common sight soaring in the North Devon skies over woods and farmland.

Common lizards are not as numerous as a few years ago but may be seen basking in the sunshine in our wilder places. They love stony areas and fallen trees to bask on.

Adders are easily recognised by the distinctive zig-zag pattern along their backs. They are Britain's only poisonous snake so avoid them and keep dogs away. They usually keep clear of us and only attack in retaliation to disturbance.

A male stonechat on bramble, a common bird of our coastal habitats often associated with gorse or furze, and a resident species.

Bee on a gorse bush. Its wonderful golden flowers may be blooming in all months of the year. Once used as cattle fodder and as a fuel and found all over North Devon, its flowers make an excellent home-made wine.

Gorse in bloom at the cliff edges where they join the sea, here seen at its best overlooking the lovely Woody Bay near Lynmouth. The North Devon coast path takes us all along these ruggedly beautiful land and seascapes.

Ilfracombe Harbour. A favourite seaside resort popular with tourists and locals, with some fine coastal walks rich in wildlife.

*Low cloud along the coast from Watersmouth. There is a feeling of freedom here
in all seasons amongst the rugged grandeur of North Devon's coastal scenery.*

Sailing on the intertidal waters of the Taw and Torridge estuarine habitats.

Surf pounding the beaches of North Devon, a fine sight reminding us of the wonderful mix of habitats in this lovely part of the West Country, as well as its attraction to tourists and locals alike. There is excellent surfing hereabouts.

From Lee Abbey looking towards Woody Bay. A superb series of hog's back cliffs takes the coastal path walker through some of the finest scenery in England.

My collie, Bracken, enjoying a dip at Lee Bay. This is good seabird country with auks and gull species breeding. There are two Lee Bays in North Devon, one at Lee village and one near Lee Abbey, close to the Valley of Rocks.

Duty Point Tower at Lee Abbey, probably the 'Lonely Tower' of Samuel Palmer's great landscape paintings. He visited North Devon around 1835.

Seal Cavern at Baggy Point. Seabirds nest on these cliffs, which feature in Tarka the Otter *by Henry Williamson.*

Guillemots. These lovely little auks, so prone to oil pollution, nest on several North Devon cliff sites and may be seen from the coast path walks during the summer.

A herring gull chick surveys the great outdoors for the first time, facing a precarious and oft-times persecuted life.

Kittiwakes on their rudimentary cliff-ledge nests. Are the souls of dead children reborn as kittiwakes? A charming bit of folklore linking us with this gentle gull.

A nesting oystercatcher amongst pink thrift. This is the sea pie or mussel picker which breeds on our coast and lives on the Taw–Torridge estuary in autumn and winter.

Razorbills, like guillemots, are auks and breed on the cliffs of North Devon's wild coast.

Wild arum berries

Autumn

Autumn Gold. Just when one thinks nothing can be more beautiful than a North Devon spring or summer, along comes autumn to make its claim.

Season of mists and mellow fruitfulness… Autumn has arrived. Summer has sort of drifted into autumn in recent years. No longer do we find sharp and positive demarcation lines twixt the four seasons yet it wasn't so long ago that they were very well defined. It used to be that one would feel a sudden sparkly chill one September morning and on would go a thicker jumper than usual. Autumn would have arrived to set the scene and we knew summer was gone other than the brief, sweet 'Indian Summers' that shorten the winters and cheer the soul.

These days climate change with, I think, a more general spread of similar weather, and storms right across the year are more or less the norm, and expected. A hundred consecutive days with rain in them was recorded here in the year 2000, and just recently a Cornwall contact wrote to me of recording 205 days passing by with only 17 days without rain! But rain or shine, a North Devon autumn is rather special, a time to be enjoyed in the great outdoors.

We all have our own favourite places where autumn colours cheer the landscape and seem to warm the chillier days with their brightness. I love to watch the changes as they occur beyond our back gate which looks directly into woodland. Sometimes subtle, sometimes swift and dramatic, depending on weather conditions, autumn always has its stunningly beautiful moments.

The wild arum, lord and ladies or parson in the pulpit, which has graced the woods and hedgerows with sheath and spadix through the summer, suddenly becomes the rigid stem and berries we all know so well, these changing from green through orange to bright scarlet as they light the lanes and wood edges with warm colour. In country lore it now becomes snakefood, a Devon name for the plant because it was believed that snakes, being the adder or viper of course, ate the berries to obtain their venom. It is not so, but in its own way this belief serves to remind us that the berries are indeed poisonous to us and thus best left well alone.

Wild arum (p.108) is also the cuckoo pint of spring, and adder's tongue, cows and calves and wake robin. As a substitute for arrowroot it was known as Portland sago, the food thought of as venereal and strengthening, with large quantities sent from the Isle of Portland to London dealers. A pure and white starch was made from the roots.

With the harvest 'in', the countryside takes on a new look so different from the newness of springtime yet with a freshness that is typically autumn. From

the days when the sickle was the first of man's inventions to be used directly for farming, to today's huge machinery, North Devon has always been farming countryside, and long may it remain so.

There is a tale about an English rector in the eighteenth century receiving a visit from his Archdeacon who was shocked to find a crop of turnips in the churchyard.

'This must not happen again,' said the Archdeacon.
'Oh, no,' said the rector, 'next time it will be barley…'

And up on Exmoor the combes are quieter without the birdsong and the hum of insects. The swallows have moved on from lovely Challacombe Reservoir, their nests in the farm buildings deserted for a while as they and their young prepare for the journey to Africa and wintering haunts. Fewer people come up here now; a walk in autumn to the Longstone menhir usually being in peaceful solitude. In the distance, beyond the reservoir, autumn mist begins to blanket the slopes, beautiful yet a warning to be sure of one's ground and location, maybe to take heed and turn back rather than be caught up and 'lost', for it is surprising how easily one can become disorientated when you can't see a hand in front of your face, literally.

And there are whinchats on the gorse. They are on the move now, having had a second brood which fledged in mid August. Indeed the adult female is feeding one youngster on the move as three others follow dad along the combe. Whinchats (p.121) and stonechats share several country names. Furze hacker, gorse chat and bush chat are among these, whilst whinchats are also known as whin lintie and fern lintie. Whinchats love rough grassland and I've found them nesting on moors, in watermeadows and along railway embankments.

The joy of any traveller wandering in North Devon is echoed in the country name for the wild clematis, for it is called traveller's joy (p.114). Also known as old man's beard, it is particularly beautiful when cascading down amongst tree branches, silvery and glistening, so lovely when backlit by sunlight, a joy indeed. Many of its local names reflect its appearance, with granfer's whiskers, old man and father time amongst these. Snow in harvest is most apt, as are gipsy's bacca and smoking cane. Gipsies and boys smoked lengths of the dry stems which actually draw well and do not catch into flame, this use also giving the plant the names shepherd's delight and poor man's friend. The plant's habit of twining amongst trees gave it the name witches' hair and maiden's hair. Look for it in such places where it lends a fairyland enchantment to the scene. Traveller's joy maybe so called for its beauty but possibly also because the leaves, when squeezed against the bruises of travellers, were said to alleviate the problem.

And now the guelder rose we saw in blossom during the summer is heavy with fruiting berries, that continuity of life I referred to earlier brimming over with fruitfulness, the mellow fruitfulness of the season, so beautifully described by Keats in his 'Ode To Autumn' (p.122).

What a glowing sight they are, enough to make us stop and stare, to be glad to have all of our five senses enlivened and in tune with Mother Nature and her bounties. The berries are taken by some bird species as food.

As for blackberries (p.123), the fruit of the bramble, well I could write a book on the subject. Collectively the various bramble species are the *Rubi* and there are some 400 different species in Britain, many of which grow in North Devon. They can be erect, sprawling or climbing, and when we find 'poor' fruits on one bramble bush, huge plum-like fruits on another, it is most likely that they are just different species.

Brambles can get around a bit, a fine example of plant migration, for not only do they spread when their long trailing stems take root in the ground, but also grow from seeds dropped by birds and mammals which have eaten the fruit.

Brambles illustrate very well the interdependence of plant and animal life, the plant well colonised by a large range of insects and birds many of whom rely on the bramble for their everyday needs and existence. The blossom and fruit season is the best time to observe, perhaps even make a study of this most interesting shrub, for the world of the bramble bush is an extremely busy one.

As youngsters we have enjoyed the purple-fingered days of blackberry picking, wonderful times. I still pick a pound or two each year for blackberry and apple pie, a part of North Devon life that is as traditional as clotted cream and conkers. A jar of home-made bramble jam on a market stall is as a magnet to us locals who are all connoisseurs of this fabulous preserve.

I've heard bramble called yeo brimmel and the fruit, mushes and even doctor's medicine, though I believe the latter is a Somerset local name. There is more to this plant than its fruit of course: the roots are used for an orange dye of rich colour and the leaves are a popular remedy for burns and swellings. Diseases were cured by passing the sick person beneath bramble arches, whilst brambles were once placed about graves, presumably to keep bad spirits away from loved ones.

It is said that we should not pick blackberries beyond Michaelmas as the devil then defiles them. In truth the fruit does tend to be 'going over' around this time with mildew setting in, but how the late summer butterflies love them, the commas and red admirals seen sucking at the juices of the mushes through their long tongues.

Snails will hibernate affixed to the leaves, wasps pierce the berries to sup from the sugary flesh and leaf miners will leave their pale trails, the larvae of the moth *Nepticula aurella* tunnelling from where the egg was laid and leaving a trail to where the moth emerged. Just a few of the myriad facets in the life of the bush that brings us such delightful pies!

The photograph on p.126 is of my dog and great friend Bracken at Beaford Bridge. I have dedicated this book to him in his memory for he passed over in April 2001 as I was writing the spring chapter. He was the best and at almost sixteen years was as full of fun as in his younger days, filling my own days with light. We did so much together and he found many things I might well have missed, knowing what I was about and always there for me whatever, through all the years we traipsed the countryside together. If I have favourite places in North Devon they were and are wherever Bracken was. A great heart and soul and what intelligence! Dear readers, if you have animal companions of any kind then cherish them, if not, there is no finer friend than a dog of the collie breed.

And what of the bracken that gave him his name. Ferns in fossil form date back 300 million years, the most primitive plants on Earth, so what a marvel it is to see a dragonfly perched on bracken in a woodland clearing or on a North Devon hillside and wonder at the time span of these ancients in terms of their incredible history.

Bracken is the best known of our ferns, spreading by its rhizomes as well as its spores. It is actually a woodland species and never grows above the timber line, that is the height beyond which trees will not grow. It is also known as brake.

In autumn a walk in such places as the Valley of Rocks can be a joy, the brack-

Traveller's joy, the wild clematis, a beautiful climber of trees and shrubs in many a North Devon hedgerow.

en now russet in colour and the last of the house martins zooming about after insects in flight. They are often the last of the summer migrants to leave our shores for the long and hazardous journey to Africa and may be seen in October, even in November in balmier autumns. Who knows, with climate change and the so-called global warming now with us, it is quite possible many a migrant may decide to remain.

In the Valley of Rocks the feral goats (p.127) wander sure-footed on the slippery slopes, interesting animals and certainly of the 'wild' type. The Lynton population are descendants of those introduced many years ago to the Valley of Rocks. There are also goats on the nearby island of Lundy, introduced in 1926 following the extinction by 1914 of goats there since the eighteenth century. At one time there were as many as 200 on the island but numbers are down drastically from the old days.

Goats were kept for milk, meat and their hair for weaving. The meat, known in some parts as rock venison, is said to be every bit as good as deer meat. The rut is in September and October. Farmers would keep goats on their land to protect cattle from contagious abortions and horses from the staggers, whilst a goat's whey is said to have valuable medicinal properties. I once watched in awe as a magnificent billy goat with superb horns killed a group of half a dozen adders coiled sunbathing on a narrow path in the Valley of Rocks, stamping in a fury and even biting one and tossing it limp and tattered into the bracken bordering the path.

The coast paths in autumn are a delight to walk, with fine autumn days often rivalling those of spring and summer as we wander the combes, the rowans heavy with scarlet berries, the purple heather on the turn and maybe a peregrine winging by. Exhilarating and peaceful are such moments when the spirit soars and all is well with the world.

A robin's pincushion (p.124) glows from its place on a wild rose stem, looking like a spiky ball of deep red moss when at its best. It is actually a gall caused by a gall wasp *Diplolepis rosae*, the female laying her eggs in the unopened leaf buds of a rose bush in May. It is the larvae's presence which causes the buds to develop abnormally, the larvae remaining within the gall through the winter, pupating in the spring and hatching in May.

Even this little world of the gall may teem with activity as other insects exploit the situation, another gall wasp *Periclistus brandtii* sometimes colonising the gall, with other parasitic species ever ready to prey on these, and so on.

Back at Braunton Marshes (p.128) autumn mists veil the land and a quiet evening stroll brings its rewards, even the cattle curious and friendly as they wander close to stare and chew the cud. There is an enchantment about these mysterious misty places at such times as a grey heron wings slowly by and the ghostly white shape of a barn owl (p.86) flies low above the dagger-shaped yellow flag iris leaves, seeking rats and mice for supper. We can watch foxes here, and brown hares, while little owls call, hidden by the mist, an eerie sound from where ancient hawthorn trees, windbent, lean over the man-made dykes beloved of moorhens and wild duck.

And on another day of dappled sunlight we may see a bird coloured as autumn in every feather of its plumage, a cock pheasant as it strolls stubble fields and marsh, wood edges and lanes across North Devon's farming landscape. It is a striking bird, all the more so because of its large size and proud, elegant way, a handsome fellow indeed, with the hen pheasants no less attractive but more quietly attired.

Not a native bird, and kept in captivity as a source of food, we do know that pheasants were well established in England by the sixteenth century. Today there are estates in North Devon which rear pheasants and hold regular shoots but the bird is well established in the wild. Indeed, even as I write, there's a pair in the woods behind my home, the female on eggs and the male coming up to the gate for grain, as she did too for a while, but she seems more wary while she has eggs to look after.

It took me ages before I realised where the nest was. Incubation will take 21–27 days with fledging mostly done with the chicks wandering about. They'll fly at 12–14 days, long before they are fully grown. I've known hen pheasants lay in nests of moorhens and woodcock nests, and have seen 20 or more eggs in one nest, but this large number was due to two females laying.

The pheasant (p.131) is *Phasianus colchicus*, from the Greek Phasis, the name of a river in Medea's country, Colchis, from whence comes colchicus, a place just south of the Caucasus on the Black Sea.

Bats (p.117) have been about all spring and summer. All British bats have special protection now as numbers have dropped alarmingly. I remember in the 1940s, the evening skies filled with bats, a wonderful sight and sound.

There are 14 bat species in Britain, with North Devon having several of these. The commonest, the pipistrelle, often lives with us in our roof spaces and is a charming, harmless little mammal. I know of eight species in North Devon that are always around but in the cause of endangered species I'll not say where they are to be found both for their sakes and for the fact that it is illegal to disturb them.

Windfall apples (p.125) are a popular food of blackbirds, red admiral butterflies and many other creatures. I grew up with several orchards around our home, great places for wildlife and for scrumping. Then many orchards were neglected and destroyed, some falling to development and urban sprawl. Now there is a revival and orchards are making a comeback which is very good news indeed. There is also an Apple Day annually with the apple, particularly its special Devon varieties, celebrated (one hopes appropriately with cider) at places such as the gardens at lovely Rosemoor, Torrington, which is open to the public and is a delightful place to visit.

My picture (p.125) also shows autumn leaves and rosehips. These and the berries of hawthorn, the crimson haws or agglets, are now being stored in the disused nests of blackbirds and the like, by woodmice for their winter caches or larders. Squirrels, jays, coal tits and other birds and animals will lay in stores for the winter, a jolly sight to watch as autumn becomes a tad chillier if no less colourful.

Bats roosting, delightful mammals now specially protected as a mammal in decline, though there are still some interesting species in North Devon.

Autumn is also thought of as mushroom and toadstool time though some of these fungi may be found at other times of the year. By now most of us will have a few breakfasts of the scrumptious field mushrooms, mouth-wateringly irresistible, and nutritious with it. Just writing about them touches off a spark and I know that even though we can buy mushrooms all year round, I shall be out along the fields again when the time comes, to pick 'em fresh as the early morning sunrise lights the fields, one's breath hangs on the morning air, and the bootprints leave tracks in the dewy grass. Now that's North Devon, too, me dears.

So let us look at a couple of fungi species that really do light the day, just two of many that add colour and interest to our nature-watching.

The beautiful sulphur tuft (p.132) is common and grows in dense tufts on tree stumps and trunks of both deciduous and coniferous trees. The sulphur yellow cap is distinctive but though the species is not poisonous it has a bitter taste and should not be eaten. It is found in all its splendour from early summer to early winter. Although the scarlet-and-white-capped fly agaric is the stuff of gnomes and fairies, I think a whole area of sulphur tuft, as shown in my picture, is truly fairy-like and magical.

The scarlet elf cup (p.133) is another late autumn-into-spring fungi and I find it increasingly in North Devon in recent years so it obviously likes the place. The bright scarlet fruit bodies, often in good numbers on dead tree branches, definitely create an impressive sight. Hereabouts they are also known as moss cups, fairy baths and have even been used as table decorations at Christmas time.

So, away from the woods and back to the tidal rivers and beaches now quiet and peaceful, unpeopled by visitors, for North Devon has still not come to grips with 'out of season' tourism. No doubt hoteliers are wintering on sandy beaches elsewhere but to the local that isn't so bad for we have the romance of the wide open spaces to ourselves.

The tide is out, and way out on the sands a bait digger toils for worms with which to tempt later the palate of bass or flounder coming in on the twice-daily tides (p.134). There's more than bass or flounder here of course, with all kinds of fish being caught, some for the table of the fishermen and women themselves, some sold in the fresh fish shops such as those in the famous Butcher's Row at Barnstaple. It can be a cold business, fishing the tides of the

Grey squirrel enjoying toast for breakfast.

rivers and the coast, as indeed birdwatching can be in these places, but by now the waders and wildfowl are returning which is what much of autumn and winter is about for those of us who pursue our quarry with binoculars or telescope. I spent nine or ten years counting waders here for the British Trust for Ornithology's 'Birds of Estuaries Enquiry', going out on Sunday mornings each month in all weathers, and the project is still ongoing. At times it was so bitterly cold I could barely focus my binoculars, my patch being from the top of Fremington Creek at the main road, out to Penhill Point, then all the way to Barnstaple Longbridge along the sand, mudflats and saltmarshes. I tell 'ee what, it could be so cold that when I got back home to warm my hands by the fire, I'd have tears of agony in my eyes as the blood thawed. Dearie me! A roast Sunday lunch never tasted better. Once or twice as blizzards blew up the Taw Estuary I've crawled into huge concrete pipes stacked on the river bank by Shapland & Petters, unable to see for snowfall, then made a dash for home when the storms abated. Today the winters are much milder, the task so much easier, and I think how did I come to choose such tough times? There 'tis.

A woman walks the beach at Saunton with a child in a pushchair (p.135). What a wonderful thing to be doing as autumn reluctantly gives way to winter and the countryside, or much of it, rests awhile. Will the child remember this beautiful moment? Maybe his or her mother will tell of it for these formative years lay the foundations of our future. The four seasons of the year are as the four 'seasons' of our own lives in many a way. I know I am visiting my own 'autumn' as we all have to do and some have done. I look back at my life in North Devon and hope I've made the most of it. In some ways I have and owe that to a few people, to Bracken, and Shepherd before him, and to the wildlife of the countryside. I owe them all as I head into winter, with no discontent.

Autumn mist heading down the combe above Challacombe Reservoir. This is part of the lovely Wood Barrow–Longstone menhir circular walk from Breakneck Hole, one of my favourites.

A whinchat on gorse, or whin, the plant giving the bird its common English name. Whinchats are summer visitors to our shores from April to September.

The beautiful scarlet berries of guelder rose, born of the blossoms shown on p.73. Autumn's fruits are an important, often vital, food for birds and some other wildlife species.

Blackberries, the fruit of the bramble, one of the most important shrubs of the countryside for its food, shelter and nesting habitat for many species.

Robin's pincushion, a beautiful gall usually found on the wild rose plant.

Autumn's seasonal fruitfulness.

*Bracken at Beaford Bridge. The Torridge River is very wooded
and beautiful, a favourite waterway shared with my dog.*

Wild or feral goats at the Valley of the Rocks. Their rut is in the autumn.

Cattle in the mist at Braunton Marshes.

An orb spider in the centre of its amazing web structure.

Part of the Lee Abbey coast walk linking the Valley of Rocks to Woody Bay and Heddon's mouth, via Hunter's Inn, an excellent refreshment stop as is the Woody Bay Hotel en route.

Cock pheasant. Resplendent in autumn's own colours.

Hedgehog. Now beginning to think about hibernating for the winter, the lovely 'fuzz-pig' looks for suitable shelter and should be welcomed to our gardens.

Sulphur tuft fungi, a veritable fairyland on old tree stumps.

Scarlet elf cup, or fairy baths.

Bait digging. Fishermen of the Taw and Torridge intertidal waters prepare for fishing on the incoming tides.

Mother and child. The wide open beaches offer peace and quiet contemplation for all ages during all months of the year.

Hogweed

Winter

Anchor Woods in winter, a scattering of snow, bracing winds and we are set for
winter wildlife, hot stews, roasts, and warm fires. Birdwatching is easy now with
the trees bare of leaves.

On the beach. Winter is only a bleak time if we allow it to be so. There is beauty in every season and now that the North Devon coast has been left virtually to the few who brave the likely cold there is every reason to enjoy the tranquillity and solitude afforded by winter.

On a winter's day I love to park up near the White House at Crow, to walk out on to the sands and on to Crow Point, the more blustery the better if it blows away the cobwebs, so to speak. Or I park farther on at the Nature Reserve car park at Grey Sands and walk over the boardwalk to the beach, to turn right towards Saunton and follow the strandline.

The wheatears have gone now, the nesting of ringed plovers long over, any skylarks we see are silent as they search the dunes and slacks for food. Upon the beach lie shells, once the homes of living creatures. Hard to believe, isn't it, that the countless millions of shells scrunching underfoot held life beneath the waves.

The vast majority of shells we find on our beaches are those of molluscs, creatures which vary in shape but all having a head, soft body and muscular foot. Of the 800 British species, most are aquatic with about 650 living in the sea. Many bivalves live on sandy beaches, including the well known razor shell (p.146) whose long rectangular valves resemble an old fashioned cut-throat razor. The muscular foot is a very powerful digging tool and, placed on damp sand, a razor shell will completely bury itself within a few seconds. But look at the beauty of such shells and consider how they are made of lime-based materials produced by glands contained in a fleshy part of the mollusc called the mantle. These shells are made up of three layers, the horny outer layer, a chalky layer beneath and finally a glossy inner layer.

The winkles (p.147) are univalves, the yellow and the orange flat periwinkles shown here being brightly-coloured varieties found on sheltered shores. Colour varies considerably according to habitat though all are associated with brown seaweeds on which they feed and lay their egg masses. The eggs hatch as crawling juveniles and may live a further three or four years. The winkles are probaby the commonest shells to be found on our North Devon shore.

Around the coast and inland, particularly planted as a hedge tree, is the hawthorn (p.148) or may. The picture shows the crimson haws touched by the first frosts of the year, the leaves are off the trees and winter is clamping down hard on the land. Hereabouts it is the aglet tree, bread and cheese, hagthorn,

Tawstock Church looks pretty in the snow but life is tougher for wildlife such as the otter.

quickthorn and whitethorn, the latter in contrast to the sloe or blackthorn. The haws or aglets feed birds and small mammals in late autumn and winter and it is common to see flocks of wintering redwings and fieldfares from Scandinavian countries stripping the berries in hard times.

The hawthorn is a supernatural tree, a lover's tree in poems, and a lone hawthorn is a fairy tree which should never be felled. It is one of the trees put around the maypole when it is carried in from the woods, a tree which speaks of fertility, the heady scent quite potent. With other magical trees, we find it carved in churches, and oak and hawthorn are often seen in Green Man carvings. Its powerful protective magic made it popular as a hedgerow tree though it is undoubtedly the finest stock-proofing species for this task in any case. Hawthorn also makes excellent walking sticks yet it is thought by some that to bring the blossom indoors is unlucky.

Hard winters see birds and small mammals feeding on berries, some finding it difficult to survive when times are extremely bitter. A reminder then to feed the birds if you are able, and to put fresh water out for them. The greenfinch in my picture (p.149) is enjoying peanuts, but water too, is very important. Our help is always rewarded by the sight of busily feeding birds in our gardens and you will be pleasantly surprised at some of the unusual species that may well come, including nuthatches, woodpeckers, siskins and bramblings.

Snow on the wood path at Anchor Woods (p.138) behind my home. Without the leaves on the trees birdwatching is usually easier, and as woodlands provide shelter and food we may well see more birds about in such habitats than we do in spring and summer. Many species flock at this time, tits and finches are often seen in good numbers so again one's chances of observing birdlife are good. If you can, get out and about. It is hibernating time for some animals; hedgehogs, dormice, snakes, frogs all hide themselves away for the winter but contrary to what some believe, grey squirrels and badgers do not hibernate, though they may well become less active. Down by the river the Tarka Trail stretches away towards Fremington, Instow and beyond in snowy remoteness, yet it is one of the busiest of all times on the intertidal rivers. This is the time of waders and wildfowl in high numbers, a great nature-watching time with always something exciting to see.

Even in a short walk we should find waders such as curlew, lapwing, dunlin, redshank, greenshank, oystercatchers, godwits, grey and golden plover, ringed plover and snipe. Herons, various gull species and cormorants will be fishing in their different ways and wildfowl such as mallard, shelduck, wigeon, teal, Canada and Brent geese, smew, goldeneye and eider may all be about. In recent years spoonbills and little egrets have become regular annual visitors and of course our resident mute swans are always about, flocking together at this time of year. Canada geese numbers have increased to over 500 strong in North Devon in recent years, quite a new phenomenon. I hadn't seen a Canada goose in my early birdwatching days yet now, on each winter's night, flocks fly honking over our roof like Odin's hounds a'calling in darkening skies, an eerie yet beautiful wild sound.

Icicles hang from the trees after winter rains, the rime (p.145) speaking of harsh conditions as we huddle by our fires. But always there is the wondering if one is missing the rare beauty of such moments, so hot drinks, plenty of layers of warm clothing, and North Devon continues to beckon us out of doors. Farmhouses and cottages scattered about the hills and valleys have blue smoke rising from them, many having retained log fireplaces as rather fitful sunshine beckons the traveller on. It is standing still that makes a body cold, better to keep the blood moving.

Hogweed (p.136) which refused to bow to winter winds stands ice-covered and sparkling, claimed by Jack Frost until the sun thaws and releases it. Now is a good time for photography, not that there's a bad time really but winter's whiteness provides numerous beautiful pictures, some unusually so.

It is a tough time for wildlife. Hibernation seems a wise decision of nature when snow and ice is about, even animals as large as the otter (p.150) finding life grim. They may take prey of all sizes now, even a mallard, itself weak from hunger, may fall to an otter especially when inland rivers and streams are iced up and the fishing is hard. Many otters move to the coast at such times, fishing the sea and estuary where opportunities are much better.

Back to Tawstock where the church lies amidst the snow. Pretty on Christmas cards is snow, some will tell you, but that's where it can stay. Otter footprints in the snow, and those of woman, man and dog, tell of animals and folk out and about for their very different reasons.

At the bend of the river a grey heron stands by Spady Gut, a tiny stream issuing into the River Taw by Tawstock woods. The tall grey bird cuts a lonely figure, winter lending it a gauntness that is less obvious in summer. Now rain is spattering, pitting the snow as if the ghosts of probing birds seek sustenance beneath the blanket of white. I walk through the tunnel beneath the old rail bridges, 'first and second iron' we always called them, black and stark against clouds building up over Exmoor way. A shrill 'peep' and a kingfisher goes downriver curving in an arc of blue and chestnut, passing Rock Park, heading for the creeks below the Longbridge on the south side where the tides leave fish in the pools for such as this lovely bird, the only touch of bright colour in the landscape. The bird needs clear water to catch fish and the river is full of ochre sediment from rains and snowfall washing into it.

'Snow on the moors,' said the weather forecaster on the radio this morning. 'Roads icy, only travel if you have to,' in a voice as cold as the weather itself. He probably had a bit of a job getting to work and it may be harder getting home. Up on Exmoor the farmers will be watching carefully, all stock in close to the farmsteads. Exmoor ponies (p.152) will have their thick winter coats, a hardy race and as much a part of the moor as the red deer and the buzzard. Back home with a mug of hot soup I wonder how they are faring. So much easier for us. But these days snow doesn't last like it used to. It's almost as if it is man-made and has that built-in obsolescence of so many modern manufactured items. Four or five days and the worst of it has gone, though we are rarely ready for it and two inches can cause chaos. It's a funny old world!

Still, the sun sets and rises just the same. Over 500 golden plover are on the sandy mud by Penhill Point. Around the corner by the old lime kiln more than 300 wigeon delight the eye along with 20 turnstones and some oyster-catchers. It will be much the same on the Skern by Appledore as well as on the Caen at Braunton. I walk in by Velator Cottages to follow the raised bank by the weir, enjoying the Knowle Water and the Caen. Water rails feed here and on the marsh dykes, lovely birds that arrive here for the winter with just a few pairs staying to breed in the county. The ponds here are marvellous for wildlife, once the actual meander of the river before it was straightened out by the high straight banks, with much land claimed for agriculture. Soon, if climate change continues and water levels rise, there'll be a King Canute situation as the tides reclaim the whole area and salt marshes reign supreme again.

Two drake mallard cackle happily (p.154). Maybe they have read my thoughts and can hardly wait for more mud and ooze to sport in. Sunshine catches their beautiful bottle-green head and neck sheen. This is their domain. This is wild North Devon and there's a fair bit of it left thank the gods. This is the true wild duck, once the males only being called mallard, bold creatures of the avian world, though some are more tame and come to our bread and other food offerings. A really wild mallard won't pander to our attentions but they add greatly to a day's birdwatching especially if observed around the year.

A moorhen (p.155) skitters across the mud, lovely stuff filled with food so vital to the existence of waders who probe at varying levels with their very different bill lengths and shapes. And here we find the oystercatchers (p.156) again, perhaps some which had nested earlier in the year on the sea cliffs. Beginners in nature-watching often raise the points that there are a lot of one-legged waders about on the estuary in winter, and what are the black-billed oystercatchers they see and can't find in field guides?

Taking the two points in reverse order, the black-billed variety are oystercatchers which have been having a good probe and haven't washed their bills clean. As for one-legged waders whilst there may be one or two about who have lost a leg, waders will stand on one leg in very cold weather to keep the other leg warm. They will then change legs occasionally which shows that there is a lot of common sense in the bird world.

Winter is of course a time when we may see unusual species about though we must remember it may not always be the time of year that causes sightings of the unusual kind, sometimes it may be that birds have 'escaped' from captive situations where they have been kept as 'ornamentals' for example.

On the Taw as I write there are two black swans (p.157). They are 'Australian' swans but did not fly in from the other side of the world and would be classed as escapees. Smaller than our mute swans they will stay around for a while then probably move on as fancy takes them.

However we do find vagrants, usually blown off course by storms and becoming 'lost', flying in wherever there's a relatively safe port of call. My picture shows a little auk (p.158) in a tidal pool at Anchor Bank, Barnstaple, as luck would have it, on the route I took with Bracken every day. It is the smallest of the auk family which includes puffins, razorbills and guillemots, and isn't much larger than a starling. It is possibly one of the commonest birds in the world with huge breeding colonies in the Arctic Ocean, but here it is a rare passage migrant and winter visitor to some coastal waters with this particular bird found the day after huge storms had hit the area. It seemed perfectly happy and unhurt in the tide pool and was gone following the next tide as one would expect.

Bracken on the Tarka Trail in the snow. He watches me, knowing his personal hearth rug is in front of our log fire.

So, keeping our eyes open for every movement, every unusual or seemingly out of place shape in a field, any odd sound, is the key as we wander the countryside, whatever the time of year.

And it is February, with winter coming to an end yet again. The joyous sunburst of dandelion-like flowers which have suddenly appeared is the coltsfoot and what a lovely sight it is in the mud and rain. Baccy plant, bull's foot and yellow stars are local names for this flower which always blooms before the leaves appear as if it can't wait to cheer us and say winter is almost over. Baccy Plant because it was smoked against a dry cough. Yes, smoked to alleviate coughing! Odd that ennit, and it is still used in herbal tobacco. Coltsfoot (p.159) leaves have been made into beers, jellies and wines, and the down was used as a tinder in the days of tinder boxes. Seek it out for its glorious sunny beauty, it is a plant doing well at present perhaps due to mild winters and I find it commonly these days.

A setting sun brings another North Devon day, and this book to a close. It is an interesting and beautiful area, North Devon, and I have barely scratched the surface of its natural history, but it is for you dear readers to delve deeper, to treat your senses to all there is to see, hear, smell, touch and taste. It will take a lifetime but as the saying goes, tomorrow is the first day of the rest of your life. A good time to start, or to continue, as the case may be. Happy nature-watching…

Rime on the branches everywhere. It can get very cold indeed but the outdoors can be fascinating whatever the weather.

145

A razor shell on a North Devon beach. Once it held life and could disappear down into the sand in seconds.

Brightly coloured winkles, the shell home to the living creature. They are univalves and found on sheltered shores.

Haws in winter, the fruit of the hawthorn or may, food for redwings, fieldfares and other birds which find harsh winters a tough time.

Feeding the birds has become part of our rapport with wildlife, bringing us closer to nature and helping birds and other animals survive hard times. This greenfinch is enjoying peanuts, a good source of energy as long as they are free from atafloxins which can kill.

*Winter can kill. Here an otter has had to take a mallard as its prey, or probably
die of hunger.*

Farming in winter is hard. Here sheep come in to be close to the farm in bad weather. TLC is the name of the game.

On Exmoor the hardy native ponies weather the cold, icy winds, their winter coats and general toughness proof against all weathers.

On the estuary it is quiet, oft time bleak, but for the birdwatcher these are the places to see thousands of waders and wildfowl at such times.

Mud, glorious mud, full of teeming small creatures which are food for the multitude of waders and wildfowl. Here two drake mallard enjoy a moment of winter sunshine on the mudflats of the Taw.

A moorhen skitters across the tidal mud beneath a bridge reflected upon it.

Oystercatchers face head into the wind as winter's iciness grips the land, water and air of the North Devon countryside. There is much beauty for us, a certain grimness for wildlife.

Unusual birds appear in the area. This pair of black swans, an Australian species, no doubt escaped from some wildfowl collection and are not true vagrants.

A real winter vagrant, a little auk, in a tidal pool on the Taw River, storm-blown but surviving.

Fremington Creek or Pill, an excellent place for winter birdwatching, with good numbers of redshank, dunlin and other species.

But we get through it! Suddenly in February a blaze of colour, sunbursts despite the cold as coltsfoot blooms, the flowers show before the leaves and we feel springtime is close by once again.

Boats in the half gloom of that strange time twixt winter and spring, the cold reluctant to give way to the warmth yet the changing of the year is inevitable as the countryside, rested for a while, reawakens.

160

My favourite places

Trevor Beer.

Map of North Devon

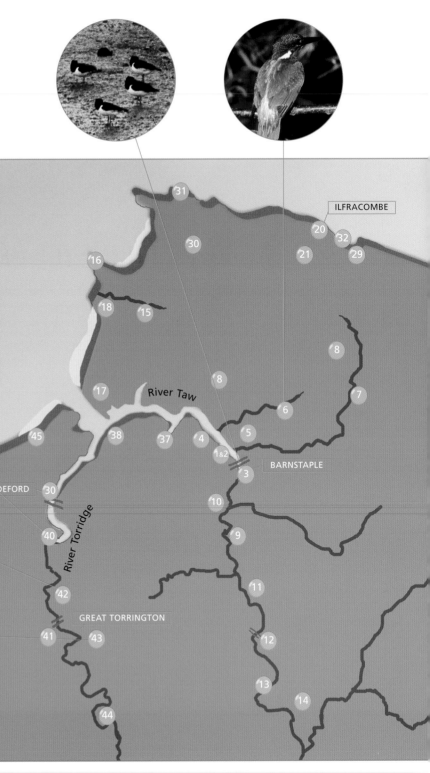

ILFRACOMBE

River Taw

CLOVELLY

BARNSTAPLE

BIDEFORD

River Torridge

GREAT TORRINGTON

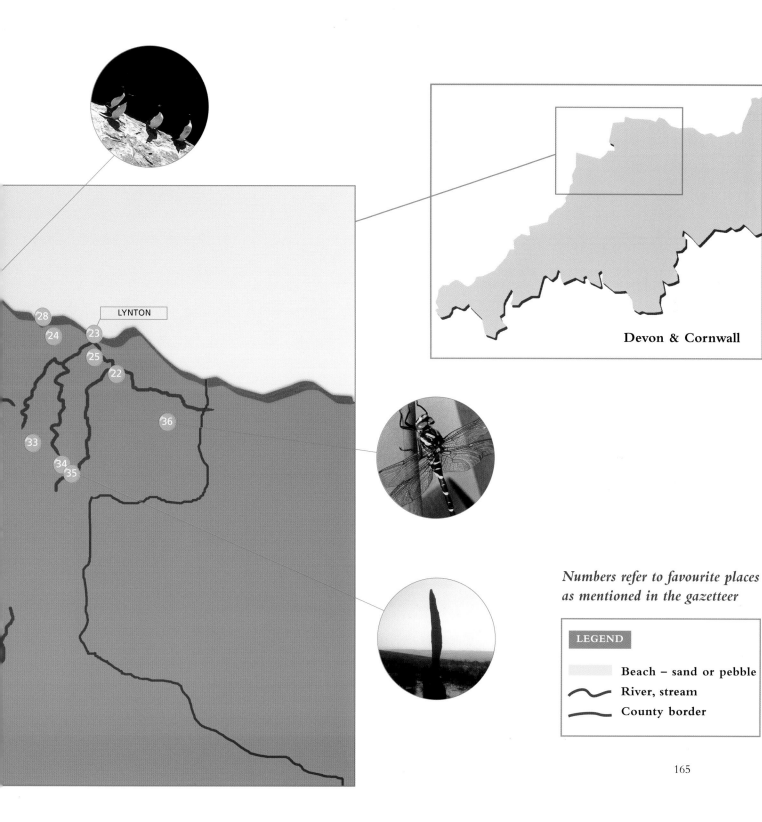

LYNTON

Devon & Cornwall

*Numbers refer to favourite places
as mentioned in the gazetteer*

LEGEND

Beach – sand or pebble
River, stream
County border

165

Where to begin?

1 Perhaps best is the most familiar of all places these days, the scene at early morning along the lane immediately outside our back gate, Anchor Woods, at Barnstaple. It is a broadleaved woodland, mainly oak with ash, gean, hazel, holly and field maple, a good wildlife location with a public footpath to the estuary of the River Taw, and into Barnstaple town. Like many North Devon woods and copses it is a haven for flora and fauna species, with always the chance of a surprise or two. It is a joy to find wild places close to urbanisation and we need to be vigilant in seeing they are not over managed or lost forever as rich and diverse habitats. Anchor Woods can be reached from the Barnstaple section of the Tarka Trail just half a mile or so westwards from Junction Railway Station car park.

2 A youngster gazes in wonder at the old Dripping Well in Anchor Woods. It is actually a natural spring issuing from the woodland bank and was surrounded by stonework in 1865 when it was part of the Bouchier Wrey Estate with its house at Tawstock, just upriver. The water in ancient belief is said to heal eye ailments, a bit of folklore proven in recent years to be true when the water was analysed and the mineral content shown to be good for the eyes! The details are currently held at the North Devon Athenaeum housed in Barnstaple Library. Wonderful stuff with much of my nature-watching done hereabouts.

3 Barnstaple on the Taw with its ancient Longbridge much strengthened over many years due to increasing volume of traffic. Here it was that the highwayman, Tom Faggus, leapt the parapet on his horse to escape capture, and here today we can view waders and wild-fowl in autumn and winter as the twice-daily tides ebb and flow. These tidal waters to Bideford are part of an English Nature Site of Special Scientific Interest (SSSI) to protect the intertidal habitat and its wildlife. On bad weather days use the riverbank walks near the town for interesting wildlife, always plenty to see.

4 Looking westwards along the Tarka Trail towards Fremington, Instow and Bideford. This is the old rail route, now a cycleway and walkway all the way to Torrington and Meeth, with walks off to villages with food and drink facilities for all the family. The Tarka Trail, based on routes taken by Henry Williamson's *Tarka the Otter*, is a Devon County Council tourism initiative which has grown swiftly, providing much needed work for locals in the area. The main offices for North Devon are at Bideford Old Railway Station. The whole Tarka Trail is about 180 miles long and includes the Exmoor and Dartmoor Two Moors Way. Excellent wildlife watching along the way in such a varied range of habitats.

5 Education is an important factor in nature conservation with nature trails providing fine opportunities for
children to visit the countryside in safety with teach-
ers, then perhaps with parents at other times. North
Devon led the way with school nature trails in the
early 1970s and here we see pupils at the Shearford
Lane Trail opening, a trail using a public footpath into
the Bradiford Valley at Barnstaple, currently an SSSI.
I spent my own boyhood here and was born nearby,
with my first den in a hedgerow when I was six
years old.

6 Bradiford Water. My earliest memories of wildlife are here, a delightful waterway, a tributary of the River Taw, flowing through Bradiford village. This is dipper, wagtail and kingfisher country with otters and virtually unspoiled farmland still in the hands of the same family as when I was a lad, and still rich in wildlife species. Best reached via Shearford Lane at Maer Top near the North Devon District Hospital. Public footpath from here to Blakewell, see local OS maps for routes.

7 About 7 miles from Barnstaple is the National Trust property of Arlington Court, once home of the Chichester family, with a fine house, carriage collection and a lake with an ancient heronry, the traditional nest area of these colonially nesting birds, the grey herons. The house is open from April to October but one may wander the delightful grounds and woodlands with lake throughout the year. Easy walking, peafowl, Jacobs sheep and Shetland ponies, lots of interesting wildlife and some fine specimen trees.

8 Marwood Gardens, known locally as Dr Smart's Garden, are a delight to visit at Marwood village, a splendour of trees, flowering shrubs and gardens in a lovely setting. Always good opportunities to use one's binoculars. I've seen golden oriole and hoopoe here over the years. The cream teas are legendary. Open dawn to dusk throughout the year. Teas are provided by the church on Sundays.

9 Tawstock church beside the Taw, with Tawstock woods riverbank walk a lovely area for nature-watching. I never fail to see kingfishers here. The church retains some fourteenth-century work and is dedicated to St Peter. Good salmon and sea trout country this, reached from Tawstock village or via Seven Brethren Bank taking the path to Barnstaple Leisure Centre and beyond under two iron railway bridges. Going by road from Barnstaple you will pass through Lake, a pretty hamlet probably so named from a small fishing lake there.

10 Much fishing is done at Newbridge by Bishop's Tawton on the Exeter road, the church in the centre of the village being dedicated to St John the Baptist. Good stained glass windows and two lovely white marble tables here. The remains of the Bishop's Palace are close by at what is now a farmhouse. The village is midway twixt Barnstaple and Chapleton stations, the latter once the best place to see wild daffodils in North Devon though over-picking saw an end to most of those. Good places to see otters on the Taw are Chapelton, and Umberleigh beyond. From Codden Hill at Bishop's Tawton fine views of Exmoor and Dartmoor can be had. Beacon fires were once lit here at 630ft.

11 Hall and Hearner Estate has wildlife links with the Devon Wildlife Trust, excellent nature-watching to be had, and a church built by the Chichester family just to the south. It is an area popular with swans, herons and gulls; just lean on a gateway and enjoy being.

12 The Taw at Umberleigh is renowned for its fishing, the pretty village clustering amidst fine wooded scenery, with Chittlehampton and Atherington villages in the vicinity. Riverbank walks provide ideal views of this part of Tarka Country with the Exeter-to-Barnstaple railway now known as the Tarka Line. I have actually followed an otter and cubs down to Chapelton from here where they emerged from the river on to a small mid-stream island to sunbathe.

13 Eggesford Weir with a salmon leaping. A lovely spot to watch these magnificent fish on their spring and autumn runs. Walk to the little church near the Garden Centre where a path leads to the river with fine alder trees on the banks. I led many walks here and gave a wildlife talk in the church itself, a lovely experience. Much afforestation hereabouts and to King's Nympton but it is not without its wildlife interest, and the surrounding farmland is very good indeed.

14 Chulmleigh and nearby Winkleigh are good nature-watching villages with much of interest on the former Winkleigh aerodrome which still has hangars and other aircraft bits and pieces linked to an old vehicle museum. Birds and small mammals live in and amongst the buses and other vehicles and nearby Woodland Trust woodlands. Chulmleigh has an ancient Old Fair Charter granted in 1253, one of the August Lammas Fairs celebrating harvest time with special lammas bread made.

Now away to the North Devon Coast...

15 Saunton and Croyde are fine coastal wildlife habitats, both extremely popular with tourists and surfers. Splendid dune systems have their own particular flora and fauna including several rare or uncommon species, a fact which has meant special protection for some areas. At Saunton there are one or two geological treasures, erratics brought by the last Ice Age from Scotland for example.

16 From the coast path walk to Baggy Point provides superb cliff scenery, seabirds including shag and cormorant, with the walk continuing on to Putsborough and Woolacombe Bay, some of the loveliest coastal views in the West Country. Bag Leap and Seal Cavern, famous Tarka landmarks, are here at Baggy along with the Wreckers Path, all as Williamson described them. He is buried at nearby Georgeham churchyard in a grave with his barn owl emblem on the stone. Myrtle Farm Cottage at Croyde has a fig tree in its garden, planted when peace was declared after the Crimean War, still bearing fruit.

17 Braunton Burrows SSSI, owned by the Christie Devon Estates, is managed mainly for its botanical interest. There is army training here at this internationally important site for wildlife which has rare orchids and many uncommon wildflowers. The area is open to the public normally, only the more serious problems such as foot and mouth disease causing it to be closed, along with the footpath and coast path network during 2001. Keeping to paths and boardwalks helps protect the vulnerable flora and fauna and should be adhered to at all times.

18 At Downend, Croyde the beautiful bedding planes of the sandstone cliffs are clearly defined. Much sea angling is done from the beaches hereabouts with conger eels as thick as a person's arm being common around this rocky coastal area.

19 And out to sea shines the lovely Puffin Isle, Lundy, a huge granite rock three-and-a-half miles long and about half a mile wide. Cliffs rise steeply to around 500ft and the total area is 1047 acres. An abundance of wildflowers and interesting birdlife makes Lundy popular with nature lovers, as does its fascinating history which includes piracy, smuggling and governors appointed by the king when it was property of the Crown. Seals frequent the island. Regular trips by ship take visitors to the island – a summer trip being a delightful way to spend a day. There is a Lundy shipping office on Bideford Quay.

20　Back to the mainland, one of the best known coastal towns is Ilfracombe with its Holy Trinity parish church. It is a hilly town, the wildlife interest mainly around Hillsborough (447ft), and Capstone Hill (156ft). Superb views can be had from Cairn Top (511ft) but do see the sunsets and sunrises from Hillsborough, here it seems as if the sun goes straight in and out of the sea. The Welsh coast is but 20 miles distant, hence the occasional red kite visiting North Devon 'for a holiday'. Plenty to hold the attention of nature lovers including breeding sea birds observable around Hele and Rillage Point.

21 Inland between Ilfracombe and Barnstaple, at Spreacombe, is the RSPB Reserve of Chapel Woods, an attractive small woodland typical of North Devon and open to visitors. Contact the RSPB Regional HQ, Exeter for permit details.

22 Watersmeet, near Lynton and Lynmouth, is a National Trust property with its popular tea rooms and shop beside the tumbling waters of the Lyn where it meets the Hoaroak Water. The riverside walks here are delightfully wooded, full of birdlife and wildflowers. Watch for dippers and wagtails here and soaring buzzards overhead. The downstream walk takes us all the way to lovely Lynmouth and the sea via the beautiful Myrtleberry Cleave.

23. The Devil's Cheeserinf is one of a number of dramatic rock formations in the ruggedly beautiful Valley of Rocks at Lynton. Mother Meldrum's Kitchen is nearby, along with the famous herd of wild goats in the valley. Sit here all day long and enjoy the wildlife of this remarkable coastal valley which so unusually runs parallel with the sea, not inland from it. The coast path walks here are magnificent, with Hollerday Hill always popular and the walk westwards to Woody Bay via Lee Abbey and Duty Point.

24. Woody Bay is one of several delightful bays set between the hog's back cliff scenery of this part of the North Devon coast, but do adhere strictly to the pathways and do not stray. Lee Abbey was never an abbey but is now home to a Christian community with holiday lets and such, and a well established estate farm. Everything here from broadleaved woodland to coastal wildlife.

25 Jenny's Leap is so named from the tragic tale of Jeenefried de Wichelhalse, who was jilted on her wedding day and threw herself from the cliffs here near her family home. This was during the reign of Charles I. Legend or truth? There is no smoke without fire but the beauty of this area lives on, one of the loveliest coastal sites in the West Country and well worth a visit at any time of year.

The superb August heather mixes with gorse around the coast but nowhere better than on the walk from Woody Bay to Hunter's Inn and the lovely Heddon Combe. Excellent car parking at Woody Bay affords the nature-watcher easy access to coast paths and a fine circular walk here, rich in wildlife and a good refreshment spot at the Hunter's Inn itself. All walks are well waymarked. I've seen everything from tawny owls to guillemots inside three hours spent hereabouts.

27 Heddon's Cleave, the lovely combe from Hunter's Inn along the River Heddon to Heddon's Mouth beach is reputedly the warmest valley in England. The lime kiln by the beach is the one described in *Tarka the Otter.*

28 Duty Point tower close to Lee Abbey is viewed here from the coast path and is thought to be 'The Lonely Tower' of the great landscape painter, Samuel Palmer, who spent time here around 1835. The birdwatching here is first class, the coastal wildflowers abundant, the sunsets magical.

29 Combe Martin abounds in delightful walks, particularly Great Hangman Hill and Little Hangman Beach, a good spot for picnics. Great Hangman (1044ft) and Little Hangman (716ft) derive their names from a 'hanged man' legend that is also found elsewhere in the UK. A sheep rustler tied a sheep around his neck for ease of carrying, sat down to rest on a stone but the sheep struggled free and whilst sliding over the stone, strangled the man. The stone is known as the hanging stone to this day.

Combe Martin itself is situated amidst lovely scenery and that generally means good wildlife habitat. The little bay is very picturesque, the western walk lovely during the evening as the sun sets. The village is basically a long straggling street of over a mile with good shops down to the harbour, and is renowned for its market gardening and fruit growing, particularly strawberries. Silver, tin and lead mines were here as far back as King Edward I's reign when Derbyshire miners were brought in to work them. The history of Combe Martin's silver makes for fascinating reading.

30 There are two Lee Bays in North Devon, one below Lee Abbey near Lynton and one at Lee village itself, also known as Fuchsia Valley. It is a lovely village with Bull Point close by in a delightful wooded setting, and I always find exciting wildlife sightings hereabouts.

31 Bull Point is about 2 miles west of Lee, famous for its lighthouse, the light being visible over 18 miles. A fixed red light below the flashing light always gave warning of the nearby Morte Stone, a much dreaded hazard, whilst during fog a siren was sounded every minute.

32 Twixt Ilfracombe and Combe Martin is Watermouth, with Watermouth Castle. Landslips occurred here in 1919 with hundreds of tons of shale and limestone falling into the sea and the road with it. Popular with boat people, the cove is quite lovely, as are the views out to Hangman Hill especially during hazy, low-cloud mornings.

And now away inland to my favourite wildlife watching spots on Exmoor...

33 I love Challacombe village and the walking to be had hereabouts. Right on the National Park boundary here with an interesting church and pleasant inn and mysterious legends. My favourite walks take in Challacombe Reservoir and Pixie's Rock, wild places where I always see red deer and foxes in broad daylight. Above the village is Breakneck Hole car park and from here there is a superb but testing walk via Wood Barrow to the Longstone menhir which stands at about 9ft tall. It is probably one of my favourite places on all Exmoor, but avoid in bad weather when rain and mist can fall in seconds.

34 Wonderful old mossy beech trees give a vantage point down over the wild moor with its heather, rowan trees, redstarts and ring ouzels. I have sat here so enchanted by the place and by the variety of wildlife to be seen.

The Longstone menhir itself when I have let darkness fall and either found my way by moonlight back to Challacombe or, on a few occasions, stayed all night beneath the stars. One is never disappointed on North Devon's Exmoor and certainly always delighted by the Longstone walk.

36 And lovely Malmsmead with its ford and old stone bridge, takes us into Doone Country with dippers, wagtails and dragonflies always there to greet the spring and summer visitor. I have to mention this pretty little place even if it is bending the rules a bit to call it North Devon. I do a lot of nature-watching here, from Barnstaple and it is not so far as to make any real difference. Good refreshments here and Exmoor Natural History Society has a good centre with all the wildlife news.

Time to head towards Torridge River...

 Fremington village is large and popular with visitors, and has an interesting church, shops and two inns. Walks from here to the newly refurbished quay guarantees interesting wildlife, especially along Fremington Pill or Creek, a tidal river with fine wader-watching possibilities when the tide is out. I have seen otters here and birds such as little egrets and many redshanks, dunlin and duck species.

38 Downstream from Fremington is Instow with broad expanses of sandy beach and dunes, a yacht club which makes for picturesque days and evenings, the boating a fine sight. Instow is a large, growing village backed by attractive wooded countryside which, with the open sands and twice-daily tides, provides an interesting mix of habitats.

39 Bideford on the Torridge. A town of character enhanced by its working quayside and large park. This is an excellent base for the nature-watcher who can head seawards or upriver as fancy dictates. I go especially to Bideford before sunset to watch the spectacular starling flock, a real murmuration as they come in to roost in their many thousands at the old bridge in the town. One of the great sights of nature is this.

40 So upstream first then, to Landcross where we find another River Yeo heading down the Torridge. I like it here for its wooded beauty and the waders on the mudflats albeit in small numbers. There is a pleasant feel about the place which is now very much linked with Tarka Country. Henry Williamson and his wife, Leotitia, were wed at Landcross Church. Herons nest hereabouts.

The old rail bridge below Canal Bridge, all part of the Torridge Tarka Route, is in a most beautiful setting, a place of salmon and sea trout, water crowfoot swaying in the river flow and an abundance of birdlife. These are places to lean on one's elbows and just enjoy being, at any time of the year. I have seen the rare night heron here and at Landcross, and always kingfishers and nesting mute swans.

41 Canal Bridge. The beginning of the Tarka story and 'canal' because this was once an aqueduct carrying water to nearby Great Torrington. Best viewed from the Tarka Trail, as my photograph shows, the bridge has three arches and is a delight for artists and photographers. It is now a road bridge to private property at Beam, but the beautiful Beam Weir can be viewed along the Trail route beneath.

42 This road bridge provides a fine arch over the Tarka Trail with excellent birdwatching to be had. Masses of wildflowers also means many butterflies and other insects. I have found glow worms along the ballast edging of the route here in high summer, a magical sight on a late evening. The Puffing Billy Inn and Restaurant is nearby.

Looking along the beautifully wooded Torridge River valley from Castle Hill at Great Torrington we can see clearly that this is first-class wildlife habitat. The Torridge tends to be more wooded along its route than the Taw and gives the impression of being a very green river I always feel. Otters are still to be found throughout North Devon with the Torridge area having a stable population of these fine aquatic mammals. Torrington is a useful town indeed for an exploration of the Torridge countryside and has many shops and much historic interest.

44 I love it around Beaford Bridge. There's something exciting, kingfishers, and lately a family of green woodpeckers out together. Seeing five together is a bit special, as was a small pack of six stoats gambolling over the bridge one evening. The church here is All Saints, whilst the Beaford Centre promotes the arts so well in North Devon. The name Woolleigh here, linked with a Saxon estate, means 'Wolves' Clearing' so the wildlife hereabouts was even more exciting years ago.

45 Westward Ho! Shades of Charles Kingsley whose statue on Bideford Quay reminds us of his writing in the town of seafaring days and Amyas Leigh. There is a Kingsley Room at Bideford's Royal Hotel. Westward Ho! beach has a fine pebble ridge and the walks around and about the coastal village are attractive. It is a modern village built after Kingsley's book was published in 1855, a company being formed to develop the area. The golf links are famous as one of the finest courses in England.

46 Clovelly is a seaside village without traffic. For the nature lover it is best reached via the Hobby Drive, a most attractive walk with woodlands and delightful views seawards. I have led many field trips here in all weathers, finding superb wildflowers and much birdlife en route. Kingsley's father was rector here, the church of All Saints being a pleasing mix of fifteenth to seventeenth-century construction and artefacts including a Norman font. Clovelly Dykes is an impressive Iron Age hill fort on the plateau behind the coast.

Hartland Cliffs and Point (350ft) is one of the great headlands on the English coast and is thought to be the Hercules Promontory referred to by Ptolemy. Always good seabird-watching here in an area rich in coastal wildflowers. Best in the spring but a place to visit at all times of the year; a lovely parish to explore.

48 Farming. The backbone of North Devon and the basis of so much of its scenery and wildlife habitats. For a while the compatibility of farming and wildlife has been strained but the signs that the two are once more coming together are good. There is an increasing awareness that we have witnessed the 'best' of the British countryside and its wildlife with environmental changes producing alarming declines in some species.

49 But as the sun sets on yet another day in the life of North Devon's people, their pets and livestock and on the wonderful world of wildlife, if this little book raises interest and awareness in the beauty that surrounds us, and has us caring just that little bit more then that's 'ansome! What you care you do, 'tis said.